HISTORIC WALKS IN CHESHIRE

by
Jim Rubery

ABOUT THE AUTHOR

Jim Rubery has lived in Yorkshire since 1975, having moved to the south of the county after being educated in the Midlands. He is a very keen participant in outdoor pursuits and has spent a great deal of his spare time over the years climbing, mountaineering, walking, skiing and canoeing, and has even dabbled with caving and sailing.

Jim started writing for the climbing press in the early 1990s, and has had a regular walking column in *Yorkshire Life* magazine since 1995, entitled 'Rambling with Rubery'. This is also now a regular monthly feature in the sister magazines, *Cheshire Life* and *Lancashire Life*. Wherever possible, Jim tries to incorporate into his walks a place of interest along the way, often a historic building or area of archaeological importance. It is from this that his love of historical places has grown, whether it is a stone circle from a prehistoric age, a ruined castle or abbey from medieval times or a relatively modern edifice from the Industrial Revolution.

This collection of 20 historic walks gives a flavour of some of the outstanding countryside and rich historical heritage of Cheshire, a county that Jim loves and where he spends as much time as possible.

HISTORIC WALKS IN CHESHIRE

by
Jim Rubery

2 POLICE SQUARE, MILNTHORPE, CUMBRIA LA7 7PY
www.cicerone.co.uk

ols Ordnance Survey® This product includes mapping data licensed from Ordnance Survey® with the permission of the Controller of Her Majesty's Stationery Office. © Crown copyright 2002. All rights reserved. Licence number PU100012932

Photos by the author, except where otherwise credited.

For Chris

Acknowledgements

I would particularly like to acknowledge both English Heritage and The National Trust for their generous co-operation in giving me access and allowing me to take photographs of their properties in Cheshire, not only for publication in this book, but for the many articles in *Cheshire Life* magazine that have featured their properties over the years. I would also like to thank the owners or custodians of Arley Hall, Capesthorne Hall, Gawsworth Hall, Cholmondeley Castle and Peckforton Castle who have made such a valuable contribution.

Many thanks go to Dave Gregory for help with preparing the manuscript and to Chris Jones for her encouragement and constant support.

Advice to Readers

Readers are advised that while every effort is taken by the author to ensure the accuracy of this guidebook, changes can occur which may affect the contents. It is advisable to check locally on transport, accommodation, shops, etc, but even rights of way can be altered.
The publisher would welcome notes of any such changes.

Front cover: The lovely gardens at Capesthorne

CONTENTS

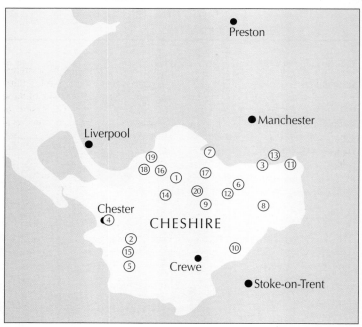

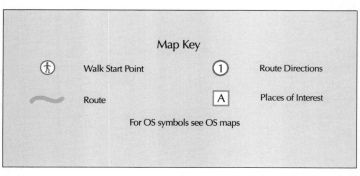

INTRODUCTION

Cheshire is a special place; this heritage county is squeezed in between the 'Land of Princes' to the west, the industrial Midlands to the south, the sweeping hills of Derbyshire's Peak District to the east and England's rugged north country. This has led to a long, rich and eventful history set in some of the country's most beautiful landscapes.

When walking, one of the most popular and rapidly growing leisure pursuits in Britain, it is almost impossible not to be aware of our historic past which makes its presence felt at virtually every fold and turn of our landscape. Whether it be a prehistoric mound or stone circle dating back to the first inhabitants of these fair islands, a ruined castle or monastery, a relic from medieval times, or a magnificent country house built and decorated more recently with the most ornate and elaborate stone and iron work, our past is everywhere. The number of people visiting these historic places has increased enormously in recent years, largely due to the hard work of the National Trust, English Heritage and the Historic Houses Association. We must not forget the numerous

Enjoying a stroll through Poynton Park

Ducks at home in the moat, Little Moreton Hall

buildings and sites in private hands, where conservation and preservation, documentation and decoration are constantly taking place. The efforts of all these groups maintain the wealth and variety of historic sites which adorn this land, many of which would have otherwise vanished by now, either under concrete and brick, through clearance schemes for forest or reservoir, or local council acts proclaiming them unsafe.

The purpose of this book is to combine these increasingly popular interests in 20 walks, which have both a scenic and historical appeal. All the walks are circular and none of them are particularly demanding, the longest walk being a little short of 9 miles. However, some of them do

venture out onto exposed sections of hillside where weather conditions can change dramatically in a very short space of time, so always be prepared. Although this book is intended as a step-by-step guide, you would be well advised to carry the relevant OS map should you require an alternative to the prescribed walk. (The maps in this guide are taken from the OS Landranger 1:50,000 series.)

In a little over 2000 square kilometres, Cheshire offers much of what is best about traditional England. There is fine walking on over 3500km of public rights of way that range from the wild, upland landscape of the Peak District to the lush riverside pastures and meadows of the plain. It also offers charming villages, friendly towns, famous stately homes, glorious gardens, fascinating museums and, of course, one of Europe's most historic and popular cities, Chester. With a history stretching back almost 2000 years to the Roman period, Chester is without doubt one of the jewels in England's well-studded crown and a joy to visit at any time of day or year.

Set gem-like in fertile pastures or perched on the banks of rivers are some of the county's stately mansions and halls, many of which are privately owned (such as Arley Hall, Capesthorne and Gawsworth). Others are in the care of the National Trust, including the Georgian Tatton Park, Dunham Massey (with its sumptuous Edwardian interior) and the

The breathtaking view from Beeston Crag.

splendid Little Moreton Hall, the finest timber-framed manor house in Britain. Many of these are packed with treasures and works of art of the finest quality. Not only do we see works from the great masters in the media of stone, paint, porcelain, wood and landscape design, but many of the sites and buildings are closely associated with some of the greatest names in English history: Richard II, Henry VIII, William the Conqueror, Shakespeare, Oliver Cromwell, the Duke of Westminster, Sir Bernard Lovell and, of course, that most famous and well-loved of our four-legged friends, Red Rum.

Over recent years there have been dramatic discoveries in the county, such as the bog bodies on Lindow Moss and hitherto unknown Roman camps and forts, all of which have allowed archaeologists to re-write part of Cheshire's early history and give a more complete and compelling picture of its past.

The chapters of this book attempt to reveal some of the splendours of this land of the 'brindled cat', with a series of walks which combine landscape with architecture, natural beauty with history, and our heritage

A spring scene at Cholmondeley

with our diverse and complex culture. It is hoped that by approaching these historic sites on foot that a greater appreciation of their being, purpose and geographical setting is gained, along with the satisfaction of reaching the place under your own steam; their contours and outline unfold before you, thus enabling you to share an experience with the ancient and ancestral people who once inhabited, developed and built on this land.

WALK 1

Arley Hall

*Arley – Arley Hall – Arley Green – Moss End –
Pick Mere – Great Budworth – Budworth Heath*

Distance:	8¾ miles (14km)
Start and Finish:	Great Budworth
Maps:	OS Explorer 267 (Northwich and Delamere Forest)

This is a splendid walk through a peaceful agricultural landscape enriched with woods and copses, lovely villages and historic estates. Despite being fairly long, it is never strenuous as it has only one short ascent of any note, but if Arley Hall and its famous gardens are to be explored along with the two villages, a whole day is required.

*Attractive cottages
in the village
of Great Budworth*

Arley Hall is a lovely example of what has been termed 'a Queen Elizabeth style' building surrounded by beautiful parkland and 12 acres of some of the finest gardens in the country. Pick Mere is a fine stretch of open water with a good variety of wildfowl and is popular for watersports in the summer months, while Great Budworth is one of the most charming villages in the county.

A. Great Budworth

This is one of Cheshire's most idyllic villages, incorporating all the elements that one would hope

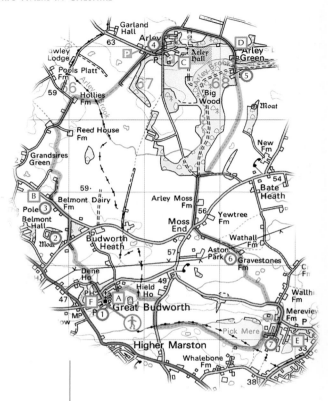

for – lovely individually
designed cottages and houses, a tiny post office, a welcoming inn, splendid views over the surrounding fields and all overlooked by the impressive sandstone church of St Mary and All Saints, one of the finest examples of ecclesiastical architecture in the county. From 1469 the village was part of the Arley estate but much of it was sold off during the 1940s. However, the village has a long and powerful history that dates back to well before the Domesday Book, in which it is mentioned as 'Budewrde', a Saxon

word meaning 'dwelling by the water'. The book mentions that the village had a priest, so one assumes a small wooden church would have stood there at the time, and notes that one of the inhabitants was a slave.

At the top of High Street against the church wall are the village stocks. These were well used up to the 1850s in order to discourage tramps and unwanted souls visiting from other parishes.

1 When facing the George and Dragon Inn, go right (north-west) along Church Street and past attractive roadside cottages. At the first right-hand bend continue into Smithy Lane, now a conservation area, and follow this as it deteriorates into a rough track. After a left-hand bend go right over a stile and along the right edge of two fields to climb a stile beside a field gate, then follow a newly made field track out to a road.

2 Cross to join the lane opposite, signposted to Antrobus and Warrington, and pass the attractive Old School House on the left. Then turn left at the T-junction and follow Knutsford Road towards Antrobus.

B. Antrobus

The village is recorded in the Domesday Book as 'Entrebus in Tunendune Hundred' (the name is probably derived from the Old French phrase meaning 'between the thickets'). Despite this, the village is fairly modern with most of the houses and principal buildings dating from the 19th and 20th centuries. The Cheshire naturalist Major Arnold Boyd, famed for his many natural history books on the area, once lived in the village.

3 Just before the Antrobus village sign go right, over a stile by a footpath sign, and along a track skirting the left edge of a field. Follow the track through a second field, past a barn, ponds and copse of trees to climb a stile beside a gate

and proceed alongside the field hedge to a farm track. Go right along this, over a stile at the end of the field and on along the right edge of the next two fields, continuing ahead where the field hedge turns a right angle, to reach a stile into another field. Veer slightly left across this to Hollins Lane and turn right along this to a sharp left-hand bend by Hollins Farm. Leave the lane here to follow an enclosed footpath round the farm, then a grassy fieldside track along the left edge of a field to reach a footbridge over a brook on the left. Once over, go through fields following the obvious path which eventually joins a broad, tree-lined track leading into Arley. Turn right through the attractive hamlet of Arley and into the Arley Hall Estate. To visit the hall continue over the cross-roads, following direction signs to the hall and church.

C. Arley Hall

Arley has been owned and run by the same family for more than 500 years; the earliest traceable ancestor is

Arley Hall

Adam de Dutton who owned lands hereabouts in 1190. The original hall was built by Piers Warburton in 1468 when he moved from Warburton to Arley. The house was enlarged in the 16th century and the original timber-framed building encased in brick in 1758, but deterioration had set in to such an extent that by the early 1800s a new hall was needed. George Latham, a relatively unknown local architect, was engaged by Rowland Egerton-Warburton to build his new house and the hall, chapel, gardens and many of the buildings on the estate date from this time, between 1832 and 1845. Rowland Egerton-Warburton wished his new dwelling to reflect something of the piety of the Middle Ages but also the grandeur of Elizabethan England. The hall has a lovely family atmosphere and contains superb plasterwork and panelling, historic furniture, a superb art collection and fine porcelain.

The hall's gardens are an absolute delight and are amongst the finest in the country. Features include the double herbaceous border laid out in 1846 which now ranks as one of the oldest in England, the avenue of pleached limes with their intertwined branches, fine yew hedges and the avenue of oaks (*Quercus ilex*) clipped to look like giant cylinders. There are also good collections of shrub roses, rhododendrons and azaleas, a herb garden and a walled garden. All in all this is a wonderful place with something of interest throughout the season; the Arley Garden Festival in the summer is one of the top horticultural attractions in the country.

4 To continue the walk, return to the cross-roads and turn right along the tarmac drive (Back Lane) and follow it round the north side of the hall and into the pretty hamlet of Arley Green.

D. Arley Green

This attractive cluster of cottages set around a village green, water pump and pond is all part of the Arley estate. The half-timbered building attached to the neat row of cottages on the far side of the green was the old school

Arley Green

house established by Rowland Egerton-Warburton to provide education for his tenants' children.

5 Where the lane veers left just beyond the pond keep straight ahead past a cottage on the right, over a stile and on along the right-hand side of two fields. Climb a stile into a third field then bear slightly right across this, continuing in the same direction across three more fields to a stile leading through a narrow belt of trees known as The Slacks. After a few yards turn right along a grassy track. This leads to a stile beside a gate with the topiary hedges of Willow Cottage and the southern drive to Arley Hall on the opposite side. Turn left down the drive to Moss End, crossing the Budworth Road at the end and continue along George's Lane to Gravestones Farm.

6 Pass alongside the farm, bearing right into a field just beyond the buildings on a rough field track. Go right, around the edge of the next field but after 30 yards turn left along a hedgeside

footpath to a plank footbridge and stile in the bottom right-hand corner. Once over these bear diagonally right across another field to reach a stile leading onto Park Lane and go left along this towards the village of Pickmere, turning right into Mere Lane at the sharp left-hand bend on the outskirts of the village, but if refreshments are required continue into the village. At the end of the lane turn right through a gap in the hedge and walk down a field, with a new housing development on the right, to reach the shore of Pick Mere.

E. Pickmere

The village of Pickmere has become fairly commercialised over recent years, with a number of caravan parks providing holiday homes for people wishing to enjoy the surrounding countryside and the watersports available on the mere.

A graceful swan cruises on Pick Mere

This sheet of water is splashed with bright colours in the summer months as the sails of wind surfers and yachts tack back and forth, sending the swans and ducks scurrying for the quieter reaches of the Mere.

7 Turn left around the Mere, moving away from the water's edge on the far side to avoid boggy sections through reeds, then continue alongside a stream draining into the Mere and follow field paths towards the village of Great Budworth, visible on

the skyline. On reaching Hield Lane turn right, ascending steadily towards Hield House Farm on the brow of the hill, but before the farm go left at a footpath sign, up a flight of steps and over a stile into a field. Walk along the left edge of this narrowing field to climb a stile at the far end; turn right over a second stile almost immediately, then bear diagonally left across a field to a stile leading onto a narrow track on the outskirts of Great Budworth. Turn left along this to join a cobbled lane leading past the church into the village.

F. St Mary and All Saints Church

This magnificent sandstone building seems incongruously out of character in such a small village, but during medieval times Great Budworth was one of the larger parishes in the country and the second largest in Cheshire, extending northwards to the River Mersey and southwards to the outskirts of Northwich. By 1130 the tithes of the parish were owned by the Canons of Norton Priory near Runcorn, who built the Norman church, but at the time of the Dissolution of the Monasteries Henry VIII gave the tithes to Christ Church College which still retains them.

The oldest part of the present church dates from the 14th century, with the solid tower, which now houses eight bells, being added in the 15th century. It is regarded as one of the finest examples of Perpendicular architecture in Cheshire.

Parking:	Discreet roadside parking in Great Budworth
Public Transport:	Cheshire County Transport Service 45 Northwich to Great Budworth, not Sundays, Tel: 01270 505350
Refreshments:	Café/restaurant at Arley Hall; inns at Pickmere and Great Budworth
Tourist Information:	Church House, Church Walk, Nantwich, Cheshire CW5 5RG, Tel: 01270 610983

WALK 2

Beeston Castle

Bunbury – Beeston – Beeston Castle – Sandstone Trail –
Shropshire Union Canal – Tiverton – Tilston Lock

Distance:	6½ miles (10.5km)
Start and Finish:	Bunbury
Maps:	OS Explorer 257 (Crewe and Nantwich); OS Explorer (Northwich and Delamere Forest) (latter not essential)

Starting from one of Cheshire's most attractive villages, this most splendid of walks takes you along quiet lanes, field paths and a lovely section of towpath beside the Shropshire Union Canal. On the outward leg the skyline is dominated by two castles perched high on the county's sandstone ridge: Peckforton, a Victorian facsimile; and Beeston, a ruined medieval gem where it is reputed that King Richard II buried gold and jewellery, and from where there is one of the finest panoramas in England.

Bunbury is one of Cheshire's lesser known gems with a lovely mixture of brick and timber housing over-looked by the magnificent cathedral-like church of St Boniface. The Shropshire Union Canal, known as the 'Shroppie Cut' to boatmen, has its most attractive section through this beautiful part of Cheshire.

1 From The Green in Bunbury walk through the churchyard and onto Vicarage Road, passing the Dysart Arms on the right.

A. The Church of St Boniface

The magnificent sandstone church dedicated to St Boniface, a west country saint, is almost cathedral-like in its proportions and dominates the village. It is believed to have been a site of worship for over a thousand years with a timber church being founded here by Ethelbald, the Mercian king, in the late 700s. That original structure may

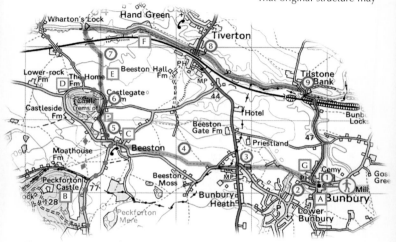

have survived until the time of William the Conqueror, but this part of Cheshire was one of the last strongholds of Saxon resistance to his rule and when this was finally suppressed the Normans dealt ruthlessly with the villages, churches and inhabitants. The current church is based on a 14th-century remodelling and contains many interesting artefacts. Unfortunately it is now kept locked during week days following recent thefts – sad sign of our times!

2 Walk down the road to the first left-hand bend then go right through a kissing gate (public footpath sign) into a field and follow a rough track initially, with the tiny River Gowy to the left. Head for the far left corner of the field and cross a plank footbridge spanning the river followed by a stile.

Turn right alongside a field hedge to reach a stile on the far side. Once over bear half left, crossing the brow of the field to reach a stile just left of a row of fir trees, and continue in the same direction across the next field, where a stile in the far corner leads onto a track past cottages. At a junction with School Lane cross and go right to a junction with the busy A49.

3 With care cross into the lane signposted to Beeston and follow this for 450 yards then go right over a stile just before Ivy Cottage (footpath sign to Beeston and Beeston Brook). Walk along the left side of a field where two stiles in the far corner can prove slightly problematic following wet weather because a drainage channel runs between them. The designated footpath now heads almost straight across the next field, but if a crop is standing walk round its right-hand side to reach a stile through the far hedge – Beeston and Peckforton Castles dominate the skyline ahead.

The splendid sandstone church of St Boniface, Bunbury

B. Peckforton Castle
(also see Walk 15)
Peckforton Castle is described by Nikolaus Pevsner, the famous architectural historian (1902–83), as 'the facsimile of a very grand 13th-century castle, correct and substantial enough to deceive anyone'. It was designed by Anthony Salvin for John Tollemache, member of Parliament for South Cheshire and later first Lord Tollemache, and was constructed between 1840 and 1851 at a cost of £67,847 9s 7½d.

4 Bear slightly left through the next field to a stile on the far side then go slightly right across a broad pasture, followed by a short field that leads to the road in Beeston and turn right through this lovely little village.

C. Beeston
This is a very attractive village, sheltered from the worst of westerly weather by the wooded slopes of the Peckforton hills and the craggy ramparts of Beeston Crag. Apart from the few privately owned dwellings, a number of cottages,

A lovely black and white half-timbered cottage, Beeston

houses and farms belong to the Tollemache family, who in the late 1800s owned over 25,000 acres and thus were the largest landowners in Cheshire. Many of the cottages date from the 17th century and display the typical character of the estate architecture with timber frames, brick infill with some later stone additions, tall chimneys and diamond-lattice windows.

It is recorded in the Domesday Book as 'Buistan' in 'Broxton Hundred', but there have been people living in the area since Neolithic times. At the time of the Norman Conquest, medieval Cheshire was already divided up into ten 'hundreds' with an attached lordship, as was much of England. A hundred is a very ancient form of land division based on a degree of coherent planning between pairings of parishes linked to early minster churches. There is a growing body of evidence to suggest that this land division may go as far back as Roman times. Following the conquests, this inherited system was remodelled and Cheshire's hundreds reduced to eight, a state of affairs which remained up to the 19th century.

5 Follow signs for Beeston Castle; the road soon climbs steadily out of the village to eventually reach the modern entrance to this splendid edifice.

D. Beeston Castle

Beeston Castle stands proud on its sandstone cliff at the northern end of the Peckforton hills, dominating the surrounding flat lands of the Cheshire plain some 500ft below. Recent archaeological evidence has proved that the site was occupied in the Bronze Age, about 800 BC and again by Iron Age settlers some 400 years later, the latter building an earth bank defence to protect their conical-shaped, timber-framed huts. The hill fort was abandoned about the time of the Roman occupation, and despite a few tantalising Roman finds at the base of the crag Beeston's history remains obscure until 1225.

You may be left panting after the short, steep ascent to the main castle ruins, but your breath will be taken away again by the exhilarating panorama from the top of

Beeston Crag which extends across the Cheshire plain to the Pennines in the east and north, the Shropshire hills in the south and the misty peaks of Snowdonia in the west. Take your eyes away from the view and you will be in awe at the magnitude of the building skills achieved almost 800 years ago. Construction was started in 1225 by Ranulf, the sixth Earl of Chester and one of the most powerful lords in the kingdom, following his return from the Crusades where he had been inspired by Middle Eastern castle-building methods. Following Ranulf's death, the castle was seized by King Henry III who regarded Beeston as far too important to be outside his control, especially with the ever increasing threat from the Welsh over the border, and so the castle remained a royal stronghold until the 16th century. During the 14th and 15th centuries the castle became rather neglected, but on the shattering of domestic peace with the outbreak of Civil War in 1642, the defences were quickly repaired and the castle regarrisoned.

A story of buried treasure has long been attached to these lofty ruins and is based upon events during the reign of Richard II when he is reputed to have dispersed

The wide views from the inner bailey, Beeston Castle

The modern gatehouse, Beeston Castle

treasure in local castles prior to his sailing from Chester in 1399. Various searches for King Richard's treasure have been made but none as yet has been successful. Many events and re-enactments take place at this spectacular hilltop fortress throughout the year, and besides having its 2500-year history to explore there is a 'Castle in the Rock' exhibition and a well-stocked gift shop.

6 After visiting continue along the road, passing the extensive Castlegate Farm on the right, before climbing a stile on the right on the north side of Beeston Crag and just beyond a left-hand bend. Go left along a broad track to its end, climbing a stile beside a gate into a field and bear slightly left across this to a stile on the far side.

E. Sandstone Trail

This is part of the Sandstone Trail, a 30-mile footpath that runs along the backbone of the mid-Cheshire ridge from Frodsham, in the north, to Grindley Brook on the Shropshire border in the south. It is one of the most enjoyable long-distance footpaths in the county and this part around Beeston and on into the Peckforton hills is arguably its finest section.

7 Negotiate the stile and continue in the same direction, heading for the tunnel that passes beneath the railway line. Once through follow a rough track along the left side of a field, over a conduit to reach the top left corner of the field where a stile gives access to the towpath of the Shropshire Union Canal. Go right beneath Wharton's Bridge, past Wharton's Lock and on along the towpath for a splendid canal-side walk.

F. Shropshire Union Canal

The Shropshire Union Canal links the heavily industrialized Midlands with the Mersey at Ellesmere Port. By 1820 business was booming to such an extent that Thomas Telford was commissioned to oversee the building of mills, warehouses, and new dock installations at the canal's junction with the Mersey. The coming of the railway in the 1860s brought a gradual decline in canal trade and by the mid-1900s this had totally vanished.

Attractive canal boats at Tiverton, Shropshire Union Canal

Thanks to the growth in the holiday and leisure industry in recent years and the efforts of canal enthusiasts, this lovely waterway is once again splashed with the bright colours of canal boats, and its renovated locks fill and empty on a regular basis.

8 On reaching bridge No 107 at Tiverton it is possible to leave the canal for refreshment. The Lock Gate Café can be found on the opposite side of the A49 while the Beeston Castle Hotel is 200 yards to the right. Just beyond the bridge is Beeston Iron Lock, unusual in that it is made from sheets of riveted flanged steel.

9 At bridge No 106 (Tilston Lock), leave the canal and go left along a quiet lane, crossing the bridge over the railway line and continuing over a crossroads into College Lane. This leads back into Bunbury, arriving in the village alongside the Dysart Arms.

G. Bunbury

Bunbury contains a pleasing mixture of brick and black and white half-timbered cottages. Unfortunately many of these were destroyed during the war when German bombers jettisoned their payloads after being turned back by barrages around Liverpool and Crewe.

Parking:	Around the Green, east of Bunbury church (grid ref: SJ569581)
Public Transport:	Mercury Minibuses Service K56 Nantwich – Bunbury; Chester City Transport Service L2 Nantwich – Chester, Tel: 01270 505350
Refreshments:	Pub at Bunbury and Tiverton; café at Tiverton
Tourist Information:	Church House, The Square, Nantwich CW5 5RG, Tel: 01270 610983
Beeston Castle:	English Heritage, open 1 April – 1 Nov daily 10–6pm; 2 Nov – 31 March daily 10–4pm, Tel: 01829 260464

WALK 3
Bramall Hall

*Poynton Park – Poynton – Dairyground –
Carr Wood – Bramall Hall – Lady Brook – Millhill*

Distance:	7½ miles (12km)
Start and Finish:	Anglesey Road car park, Poynton Lake (grid ref: SJ923847)
Map:	OS Explorer 268 (Wilmslow, Macclesfield and Congleton)

Prior to changes in the local government map in 1974, Bramhall and its splendid hall resided squarely in Cheshire. Poynton, bitterly opposed to being annexed to Greater Manchester, fought the scheme and won the right to stay in the county. This pleasant walk ignores invisible boundaries and once more joins together, by field, stream and track, these two neighbours and visits one of England's finest treasures along the way.

Poynton Lake

28

Poynton, once a coal-mining settlement, is now a commuter village with attractive parkland and a fine lake. Bramall Hall was described by Nikolaus Pevsner, the famous architectural historian (1902–83), as being 'one of four of the finest black and white timber-framed houses in England', while Bramhall Park forms a perfect setting for the hall and extends to over 60 acres of landscaped grounds.

1 From the car park at the north end of Poynton Lake, turn right along Anglesey Drive, passing desirable residences and well-manicured gardens (these are on the outskirts of Poynton).

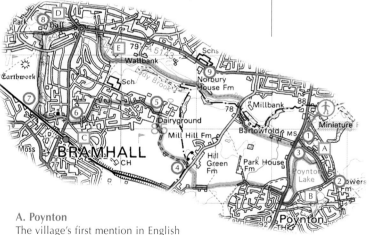

A. Poynton

The village's first mention in English history occurs in 1248 when the settlement is referred to as 'Poninton'. Over the ensuing years its importance grew considerably under the influence of the Warren family, the manorial lords of Poynton, whose manor courts not only conducted local business but Stockport's too. From the late 1500s through to the 1930s, Poynton evolved as a coal-mining village, and under the management of the Vernon family local pits became some of the most productive in the county, contributing two-thirds of Cheshire's total coal output in the early 1900s. From 1915 onwards coal production began to decline, and Poynton's last (and newest) pit, the Lawrence, finally closed in 1935. Today, the casual visitor will see little evidence of Poynton's 400-year association with coal; the spoil heaps, winding gear and network of railways have gone, and the rows of colliers' cottages are now highly desirable residences in this expanding, up-market village.

2 At the end of Anglesey Drive go right for 70 yards to a pedestrian gate on the right leading onto a track through Poynton Park, but where the track swings left continue ahead to reach the lake.

B. Poynton Park

Several well-placed benches along the shore afford splendid views across this tranquil stretch of water that is home to numerous wildfowl and waders including swans, coots, moorhens, mallard, Canada geese and great crested grebes. This local beauty spot once formed part of the Vernon family estate on which stood The Towers, the family manor house, which has long since been demolished.

3 Go left to join a good footpath along the lake shore and at the far end turn right along South Park Drive to reach the A523. Cross with care, turn right on the far side (just beyond the Bull's Head pub), where Vicarage Lane is entered. At the far end bear slightly right across a grassy island, followed by a road, onto a bridleway running parallel with a road. Proceed along a surfaced track and keep left where this forks by Phillips Bridge to join a rough, enclosed track known as Lower Park Road. Follow the track between fields then past cottages, but 50 yards beyond a flat-roofed house on the right, turn right over a stile and along the right edge of a field. Climb a stile at the far end, go

left alongside a hedge to another stile, where the hedge and a rustic fence bifurcate, and continue in the same direction to a road.

4 Cross onto the access drive leading to Birch Hall Farm (a kennel, cattery and menagerie for all manner of animals), and once past this continue along the drive as it swings gently round to the right; there are splendid views to the right over Lyme Park and the Peak District hills. The drive skirts the edge of one of two golf courses in Bramhall then, at a cross-roads of tracks in front of the drive to Further Dairyground Farm, turn left along the right edge of Dairyground farmyard and towards houses in Pownall Green.

C. Bramhall Township

Burdett's Cheshire map of 1777 shows three hamlets in Bramhall township: Siddal Houses, Bramhall Green (perhaps the site of the original village) and Pownall Green. The latter was owned by the Pownall family who bought the land from the Davenports of Bramall Hall at some point in the early 1700s and then built a hall here sometime in the mid-18th century. Peter Pownall's diary of farming in this period has survived and suggests that various parts of the estate were named according to the type of farming taking place; Barley Ground, Dairyground and Further Dairyground are typical examples.

5 Eighty yards beyond the farmyard turn left onto an enclosed footpath between houses, and proceed along Camberley Close. At a T-junction with another road go left and follow it round to the right. Go past the first turning into Sunningdale Mount but at the second go left along it for 20 yards then turn right onto an enclosed footpath that leads into Northcote Road. Walk along this, continue into Dairyground Road and past The Shires Hotel, then go right along Ladythorn Road to a junction with a main road.

6 Cross with care. Turn right to reach Robin's Lane and turn left along this, passing to the left of Bramhall parish church. Immediately before the road passes beneath the railway line turn right onto a broad footpath running to the rear of the exclusive Forbes Park, an attractive, individually designed housing complex which recreates the style of an English manor estate with gatehouses and even a casteleated mansion.

7 The path swings round to the right and through the leafy glades of Carr Wood before reaching a road, which is crossed. Continue on the footpath through the grounds of Bramall Park. Walk past a car park, cross a surfaced track and proceed on to reach the splendid Bramall Hall.

D. Bramall Hall

Nikolaus Pevsner judged Bramall Hall to be one of the four best timber-framed mansions in England; the architect Henry Taylor wrote in 1884 that 'For charm of situation and picturesqueness in style of character, Bramall Hall is unrivalled amongst the many interesting black and white mansions of Cheshire' – words that still hold true today. A hall has stood here since at least the 14th century and some early work still survives, but the main visible features are essentially Tudor, with massive oak timbers creating the main outline of the building and plaster-covered raddles and daub forming the infills. Visitors can marvel at this outstanding Cheshire 'magpie' and wander through rooms that span over 600 years of history, enjoying varied architecture, period furniture and paintings, fine Elizabethan plaster ceilings and nationally important 16th-century wall paintings.

This magnificent manor house, one of England's finest treasures, is however no stuffy museum. Stockport Metropolitan Borough Council, who took over the hall in 1974, have a policy to bring its wealth of heritage alive with special events, concerts, tours and workshops. It can be hired for corporate events and is a popular civil

Bramall Hall, east front

marriage venue with receptions being held in the splen-did Banqueting Hall.

8 After visiting, descend through the grounds to reach the Lady Brook and turn right along this, exiting from Bramall Park at the attractive black and white East Lodge. Go right along the busy A5102 for a few yards then cross via a grassy island into Bridge Lane. Walk past shops to reach pedestrian lights, cross to the far side then bear left through a rustic fence onto a track signposted to 'Happy Valley'. The track runs alongside the Lady Brook and through grassy meadows before swinging left to a new rustic footbridge over the brook. Once over turn right alongside the brook.

E. River Brame

In medieval times the brook was known as the River Brame; its reliable fresh water supply and abundant fish stocks probably had a profound influence on the siting of Bramall Hall. Today its banks are covered in wild flowers and its waters overhung by shady trees, providing numerous habitats for many species of animal, bird and insect.

The Lady Brook near Bramhall

9 At the far end of a long grassy meadow the path is forced left, away from the brook, but after 20 yards turn right over a footbridge spanning a small stream and climb a stile onto a footpath signposted to Chester Road. Walk along the left edge of fields to reach the road. Go right along this and over Millhill Bridge then, 150 yards beyond this, turn left into Mill Hill Hollow, a surfaced lane passing houses. At the far end join a footpath to the left of a house, and continue through a belt of trees to join an enclosed path through fields that crosses Poynton Brook before reaching the A523. Cross with care to steps on the far side leading to Poynton Lake and go left along this back to the starting point of the walk.

Parking:	See Start and Finish
Public Transport:	Services X1, 391 and 392 Macclesfield – Manchester and 190 and 390 Bramhall – Stockport, Tel: 01625 534850
Refreshments:	Pubs in Poynton and Bramhall; café at Bramall Hall
Tourist Information:	83 Park Lane, Poynton SK12 1RD, Tel: 01625 874225. Graylaw House, Chestergate, Stockport SK1 1NG, Tel: 0161 474 3320
Bramall Hall:	Good Friday – Sept: Mon – Sat 1–5pm, Sun and BH Mondays 11–5pm. Oct – 1st Jan: Tues – Sat 1–4pm, Sun and BH Mondays 11–4pm. 2nd Jan – Good Friday: weekends only 12 noon–4pm, Tel: 0161 485 3708

WALK 4
Chester

Eccleston – River Dee – Earl's Eye – St John's Church –
City Walls – Duke of Westminster's Drive – Eccleston

Distance:	8½ miles (13.7km)
Start and Finish:	Eccleston (alternatively join the walk at any point in Chester where there is access to the city walls)
Maps:	OS Explorer 266 (Wirral and Chester/Caer)

This is a splendid full day's walk from Eccleston (the most charming of the Eaton estate villages) alongside the serene waters of the River Dee into the magnificent Roman city of Deva, or Chester as we now know it. The delights of the city are then viewed from the high vantage points afforded by the city walls, the most complete in England, before returning to Eccleston along the tree-lined Duke's Drive.

The River Dee, once of great strategic importance between Wales and England, is now a lovely recreational waterway for pleasure craft, canoeists and anglers. The ancient city of Chester has quite rightly been described as 'The Historic Jewel of England's northwest', while Eccleston, the gateway to the county's largest estate, is an absolute jewel in its own right.

1 From the river end of the car park turn left through a kissing gate onto the riverside footpath.

A. Marches Way
This is part of the Marches Way, a 204-mile long-distance footpath traversing the Welsh border between Cardiff and Chester, the first 25 miles being within

35

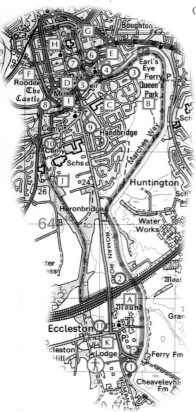

Cheshire. The walking is flat and easy through the riverside meadows but with numerous stiles to negotiate. Prior to the building of the weir near the Old Dee Bridge in Norman times, this part of the river was tidal, and even today the occasional high tide does breach the weir causing the waters to back up along this stretch and sometimes flood the meadows.

2 After passing beneath the busy A55, peace once again returns with only the chirpy sounds of birds, the whisper of the wind along the valley and the occasional splash of a rising fish as it breaks the dark, silent waters of the Dee in search of insects. On the out-skirts of the city, the moorings of Chester Sailing Club are passed on the opposite bank before the river cuts a gentle curve round a section of water meadows known as the Earl's Eye.

B. Wildlife Haven

Earl's Eye is not only important for its prime agricultural land, but as a haven for a variety of wildlife includ-ing bog-loving plants like the yellow iris, numerous birds, lots of insects and a colony of weasels. These are fierce little creatures which live on other small ani-mals, particularly mice, voles and rabbits, all washed down with a bird's egg or two. This animal is weasely recognisable from its close cousin, the stoat, which is stotally obvious!

3 At the far end of the meadows, pass through a white painted iron gate and along a paved footpath to the Queen's Park Footbridge.

C. Footbridge

This elegant iron suspension footbridge was built in 1923, replacing the original, which was opened in 1852 to allow city folk easy access to the suburb of Queen's Park. A piece of coiled steel used in its construction has been made into a paper weight and now resides in the Town Hall.

4 Cross the bridge onto the city side of the river and climb steps on the far side towards the red sandstone church of St John the Baptist.

D. King Harold of Chester?

To the left, at the base of the steps, is a tall sandstone building known as the Anchorite's Cell. Local legend has it that the Saxon King Harold did not die at the Battle of Hastings but escaped to Chester where he spent the rest

Enjoying the peace and quiet of the River Dee

of his life as a holy hermit (an anchorite) in this very building; and that's 'one in the eye' for Sussex!

5 At the top of the steps lie the ruins of Chester's first cathedral, St John's.

E. Church of St John the Baptist

This church dates from Norman times and its towering arches give some indication of the size of the original structure. After the Dissolution of the Monasteries in 1540, part of the church was allowed to fall into decay.

6 Beyond the ruins, veer left towards the Roman amphitheatre, passing Chester Visitor Centre on the opposite side of the road.

F. Deva

Chester began life around AD 79 when the 20th Legion of the Roman Army established a fortress here in order to protect the land to the east of the river from marauding Welsh tribes and northern Celtic Brigantes. They christened the fort Deva Castra, or Deva, after the River Dee. Its position, on a low sandstone bluff set within a loop in the river, was chosen because the Dee could be bridged here and also because, during Roman times, the river was navigable to this point. It is believed that the fortress housed up to 6000 men at times and there is still much evidence of Roman occupation today, including the amphitheatre, the harbour wall, the defensive wall of the fortress and the grid-like street pattern of the city.

7 Walk through the amphitheatre, past the Roman Gardens with its columns and hypocaust, beneath the arch at Newgate and climb steps on the far side to gain the City Walls. Turn left here and follow the ancient walls all the way round the city, taking advantage of the numerous opportunities to alight from them in order to explore more thoroughly.

G. City Walls

One of the finest ways to view the delights of Chester is from the elevated vantage points afforded by the walls, looking inwards along the busy streets lined with magnificent black and white buildings or outwards over beautiful Cheshire countryside and the misty sweeps of the Clwydian hills. Eventually the walls swing south, past the Roodee (Chester's racecourse) and along the old Roman Harbour Wall. This is a remnant from the time when Chester was the principal port in north-west England, prior to the silting up of the Dee.

A view from the city walls along Tower Wharf on the Shropshire Union Canal

H. Chester Cathedral

One of the not-to-be-missed sights in Chester is its splendid red sandstone cathedral which stands on the site of a 10th-century Saxon church, originally dedicated to the Mercian princess St Werburgh, who died around 707. She was a pioneer in the founding of monasteries in the region and, following her death, her shrine became the focal point of medieval pilgrimages.

The earliest documented evidence for the church dates from 958, but by 1092 the building had become a

39

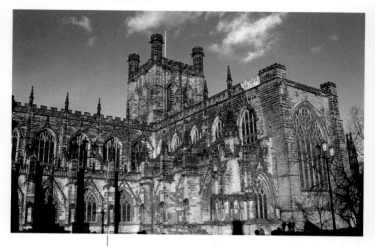

Chester Cathedral

Benedictine Abbey and remained under that order for almost 500 years. Following Henry VIII's Dissolutionment Act in 1540, the Abbey Church became the cathedral of Chester Diocese and the seat of a bishop. The dedication also changed to that of Christ and the Blessed Virgin.

The buildings that stand here today retain much of the original medieval ground plan, but numerous changes have taken place over the centuries to the buildings themselves, with Gothic and Victorian architecture now overwhelming much of the original Norman church. The cathedral houses possibly the finest 14th-century carved choir stalls in Britain, and the Lady Chapel contains part of a stone shrine which once held the remains of St Werburgh.

8 Shortly after passing the castle the walls cease and a short section of road is followed before crossing the Old Dee Bridge.

I. Bridging Point
This solid, seven-arched structure was until the 19th century the only bridge spanning the Dee at Chester. Recent

archaeological evidence indicates that its origins may go back as far as Roman times, but there was a bridge spanning the Dee here during the reign of King Edward the Confessor, as chronicled in the Domesday Book. Records also mention a number of timber bridges being washed away in floods during the 13th and 14th centuries.

There are fine views from its eastern parapet towards the city and over the weir with its salmon leap. The weir was reputedly constructed by Earl Hugh in the 11th century to provide water power for his Deeside mills and by the 16th century its water powered at least 11 mills: six for grinding, three for fulling cloth and two to lift water from the river to the city.

9 On the far side, turn right through Edgar's Field (the site of the remains of a Roman shrine dedicated to the god Minerva) then walk along a riverside track before turning left just beyond the house called 'Nowhere' into River Lane. At the far end, cross the lane and bear right along Overleigh Lane, veering left at the end along a short drive leading to

Mellow sandstone arches of the Old Dee Bridge span the river at Chester

the gatehouse and fine wrought-iron gates which give access to the Duke's Drive.

J. Duke's Drive

On the OS map this is called 'Chester Approach', but it is known locally as the Duke's Drive, being one of the main tracks from Chester to the Duke of Westminster's mansion, Eaton Hall, just south of Eccleston.

10 Walk along the tree-lined drive, bearing left at the end to join the old Roman road leading into Chester and go right along this into Eccleston village.

K. Eccleston

The village is composed of a fascinating variety of the most charming and well-kept buildings, centred around the huge parish church of St Mary the Virgin. This was rebuilt by the first Duke of Westminster at his own expense in 1899, the year of his death.

11 Turn left into the village and follow the road round to the right, past the conical towers of Eccleston Paddock, before turning left just in front of the entrance drive to Eaton Park, and head back to your starting point.

Parking:	Small riverside car park south of Eccleston (grid ref: SJ414622)
Public Transport:	Chester City Transport service 14: infrequent and no Sunday service, Tel: 01244 602666
Refreshments:	All tastes catered for in Chester
Tourist Information:	Town Hall, Northgate Street CH1 2HJ, Tel: 01244 318356. Chester Visitor Centre, Vicars Lane CH11XQ, Tel: 01244 351609. Chester Railway Station, Station Road CH1 3W, Tel: 01244 322220

WALK 5

Cholmondeley Castle

*Cholmondeley Arms – Cholmondeley Park and
Gardens – Castle Hill – Croxton Green – Chorley*

Distance:	7½ miles (12km)
Start and Finish:	Cholmondeley Arms (grid ref: SJ552505)
Maps:	OS Explorer 257 (Crewe and Nantwich)

This easy, but fairly long walk on the flat lands to the east of the Bickerton and Peckforton hills visits one of the county's most popular gardens at Cholmondeley. Then it crosses lush meadows and verdant fields where the renowned trainer Ginger McCain now casts a knowledgeable eye from Bankhouse Farm over tomorrow's Red Rums.

The Cholmondeley Arms is a wonderful inn, elegantly converted from a village school, while Cholmondeley Castle Gardens are regarded by many as being one of the most romantically beautiful gardens in England.

It is difficult to put an exact mileage to this walk due to the numerous extensions that are possible. If the chapel, mere, gardens and walks around Castle Hill are included, an extra couple of miles can easily be added to the total.

A. Village School

The Cholmondeley Arms served as a village school, renowned for its italic writing, for well over 100 years until it closed in 1982. Six years later the building was carefully converted into the bright and airy pub that stands here today. It still retains a little of the old school-hall feeling, with chunky radiators and lofty ceilings, but the cuisine

couldn't be further
removed from those stodgy dinners of long ago – to which
its numerous awards bear testament.

1 From the Cholmondeley Arms, cross with
care the busy A49 and turn into the road
opposite, signposted to Cholmondeley Castle
Gardens, and walk past a lane leading off to the
right towards the lovely black and white half-timbered Shingle Cottages and Estate Office. On
reaching the tiny thatched lodge and entrance
drive into Cholmondeley Park, go right to eventually reach the ticket booth. (If the park and gardens are not open, continue along the road for
1½ miles, rejoining the walk at point 5.)

2 The drive swings gently left through lush parkland and over a bridge spanning Deer Park
Mere, which has a good footpath all the way round
it and adds a fine waterside section to the walk. A
rustic footbridge, almost at the far end of the mere,
leads onto a small island with a wooden jetty pro-
jecting out into the languid waters of the lake. The
most serene of English landscapes can be seen
from here, with geese and ducks cruising across the
placid waters and, on the far side of the mere, the
Windsor-like towers of Cholmondeley Castle
framed between magnificent cedars of Lebanon
and mighty oaks. After circumnavigating the mere,
cross the drive and head towards the castle, crossing flat, grassy meadowland, that is used as a car
park, and the cricket pitch over to the right.

B. Quintessential England

There is a flourishing cricket club here, which is hardly
surprising when you consider the wonderful setting for
the pitch. The club celebrated its centenary in 1987.

3 On the far side of the meadow, pass through the
white Badminton Gates and into the gardens.

Cholmondeley Castle

A perfectly formed rose from the gardens at Cholmondeley

C. Cholmondeley Castle and Gardens

Whatever the season there is always something to delight (apart from winter when all is closed to the public), from the earliest spring bulbs through to the magnificent reds, oranges and golds of the autumnal foliage. Rose gardens, herbaceous borders, sparkling streams, shady woodland, sweeping lawns, water gardens and so much more are here for all to enjoy, from the casual Sunday gardener through to the most avid botanist. Children will find Scotch Farm particularly enjoyable with its goats, llamas, shetland ponies, pigs, sheep and cattle.

4 After visiting, follow the exit drive out past the plant sales area to the road.

5 Turn right, passing the extensive buildings of Castle Farm on the left, before reaching the goods entrance to Cholmondeley on the right. There is a footpath sign to Croxton Green; follow this. This leads round the northern slopes of Castle Hill before reaching a crossroads of tracks by Scotch Farm. Turn left along a rough track to a stile on the right, just beyond the gardens of Park House. Once over, head down a field, bearing steadily away from the right-hand fence, to reach a less than substantial plank footbridge spanning a small stream at the bottom (it took my weight of 13 stones but I didn't linger to ponder the flexion qualities of wood!). Climb steeply over the brow of the next field and follow the line of overhead power cables down the field to a gate at the bottom.

D. Red Rum

You have probably noticed that this is serious horse country and since the arrival of Ginger McCain and family to the Cholmondeley Estate, it has probably become seriously serious. Many of the fences in the area bear testament to this as do the deep hoof marks in many of the fields. If you feel the ground vibrate to the thud of galloping horses I suggest you tuck yourself tightly against a hedge or fence and admire the grace and power of Mr McCain's charges. You never know, you may spot a future National winner or, if it were possible, another Red Rum!

6 Walk along the left edge of two fields to a gateway on the left. Pass through this and head along a narrow meadow, with Coronation Wood to the right, to reach a stile to the right of a well-scuffed field gate and then, once over, turn right alongside the wood. The walk continues through a pair of iron field gates, over a drainage channel and on along an indistinct grassy field track with fine views over the Bickerton and Peckforton hills to the left. Climb a stile at the end of the meadow, just in front of Sicily Oak Farm, and turn right along the

Horses grazing in Cholmondeley Park

farm access drive to a T-junction with a lane. Go right along this, past Croxton Green Farm to join a rough, muddy track, but turn left 150 yards beyond the farm onto a subsidiary track leading into a field. Go right along the edge of this and the next field to eventually join the A49, which is adjacent to the large, white-painted buildings of Higginsfield House and turn right along this for 400 yards. Just before the lovely mellow sandstone building of Beeston Lodge, cross to a stile on the opposite side of the road and beside a junction with a lane.

7 Bear diagonally right, up a field, passing two small ponds on the right, to a stile beside a gate at the top of the field with the buildings of Dowse Green Farm over to the left. Continue in the same direction across the next field to a stile on the far side. Once over, walk along the right edge of two fields, round the left edge of a third to a stile beside a field gate in the corner, then head across the middle of the next field to a stile in the diagonally opposite corner and a junction with a lane. Turn

Sicily Oak Farm

right along the lane, passing the entrance to
Wallstone Farm which, like many farms in the area,
is part of the Cholmondeley Estate.

E. Chumley

There are reputed to be 24 different ways of spelling
Cholmondeley (pronounced Chumley) but it originates
from the Saxon term 'Calmunds Lea', meaning a meadow
pasture. There is no actual village here, only a scattering
of houses and farms surrounding Cholmondeley Park and
covering an area of approximately two square miles.

8 Just before Breeze Hill Farm, go left over a stile
beside a gate and along the right edge of two
fields (a double stile through the separating hedge
is about 15 yards out from the field corner), passing
to the right of overgrown ponds. Just beyond the
ponds climb a pair of stiles separated by a drainage
ditch then bear slightly right across the next two
pastures to a junction with a road near Chorley
Bank. Turn left and walk up the road for 80 yards to
a stile on the right, just before a small bridge. Move
along the edge of the field, with a stream for company, to a wooden pedestrian gate in its far corner.
This leads onto a narrow lane which is followed to
the left back to the Cholmondeley Arms.

Parking:	If you intend to use the Cholmondeley Arms you may park in the pub car park. If not, use rough verge parking opposite.
Public Transport:	Service K71 Nantwich – Whitchurch via Wrenbury. Mercury Minibuses, Tel: 01829 260397 or Cheshire Busline on 01270 505350
Refreshments:	Inn at start; café at Cholmondeley Castle Gardens
Tourist Information:	Church House, The Square, Nantwich CW5 5RG, Tel: 01270 610983
Cholmondeley Gardens:	Various events throughout year; for information and opening call the secretary, Tel: 01829 720383

WALK 6
Nether Alderley Mill and Hare Hill Gardens

*Wizard car park – Hare Hill – Vardentown –
Hocker Lane – Nether Alderley – Alderley Edge*

Distance:	7 miles (11.25km)
Start and Finish:	The Wizard car park, Macclesfield Road, Alderley Edge
Map:	OS Explorer 268 (Wilmslow, Macclesfield and Congleton)

Heading south from the urban sprawl of Greater Manchester, Alderley Edge, with its bonnet of trees and abundance of footpaths, is the first tract of real countryside one comes to. Besides the Edge with its extensive vistas, the area boasts historical mining remains stretching back to the Bronze Age, ancient legends, attractive countryside, lovely gardens at Hare Hill, fine houses at Nether

The tea shop at the Wizard car park

Alderley, a beautiful 14th-century sandstone church and a splendidly restored corn mill that is one of the oldest buildings in this part of Cheshire. All of these combine to create an outstanding walk that needs a full day if all the places along the way are to be fully explored.

1 From the Wizard car park, walk towards the Information Centre and turn right along a broad track signposted for Hare Hill, but where this begins to swing gently left after 200 yards, bear right onto an enclosed footpath through the middle of a field. Cross a track by Edge House Farm, continue past the farmhouse, climb a stile and walk down the right-hand edge of a field with fine views ahead towards the hills of the Peak District. In the bottom corner go right over a stile, walk along the edge of the next field for 40 yards to a stile on the left and join a sandy track between fields.

2 At the far end, climb a stile directly ahead onto an enclosed footpath, ascend to a stile on the brow of a

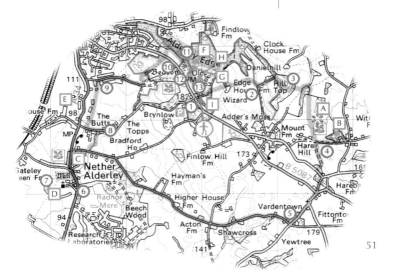

51

hill, then go left round the edge of a field and past two ponds to a stile beside a gate. Proceed round the left side of the next field to a stile and, once over, go forward a few paces onto a footpath that bears rightward through Clock House Wood. This newly constructed footpath is not shown on the OS map but it eventually descends steps, crosses the corner of a meadow then enters the National Trust's Hare Hill Estate.

A. Hare Hill Estate

The Hare Hill Estate consists of 284 acres of rolling parkland, broadleaf and mixed woodland, several small ponds and a lovely walled garden surrounded by many species of azalea and rhododendron. Colonel Brocklehurst, who lived at Hare Hill House (now a private dwelling), presented it to the National Trust in 1978. Notice the Cheshire parkland metal hurdle fences as you walk through the estate, a historically important feature of the local landscape.

The Walled Garden, Hare Hill

3 Follow the broad, leafy footpath through Danielhill Wood. On the far side go left round

the edge of a field to enter Alder Wood and on exiting from this turn right up the edge of a field with the wood to your right. Climb a stile at the top of the field and bear diagonally left across an undulating pasture, passing to the right of an attractive pond, to an iron kissing gate. Once through, bear slightly left through a large meadow scattered with fine mature trees (waymarkers) to reach an iron gate leading into the car park of Hare Hill Gardens.

B. Resplendent Blooms

The gardens, including the Walled Garden, which cover approximately 10 acres in all, were laid out at the same time as Hare Hill House was built in 1820. The Walled Garden was originally developed as a cottage garden for growing vegetables and cut flowers for the house, but Colonel Brocklehurst changed it to a dedicated flower garden in the latter years of his life. Though well worth a visit at any time of year, these attractive gardens are at their most resplendent during May when the azaleas and rhododendrons are in full bloom.

4 To continue the walk, cross the car park to the ticket kiosk and walk along the access drive onto the Prestbury Road. Turn left along the road for 100 yards then, at a left-hand bend, cross and go right into a quiet lane through woodland. Cross the awkward junction with the Macclesfield Road into Birtles Lane with care and follow this first past the old School House, then Over Alderley Methodist Chapel and finally an attractive row of cottages at Vardentown.

5 At a cross-roads a little further on, turn right into Hocker Lane passing occasional cottages and farms. At a cross-roads at Shawcross, continue ahead, still on Hocker Lane (which is now a broad, partly surfaced track). Proceed along the lane for approximately one mile to a junction with another

track (Bradford Lane) and here go left to a stile on the right, opposite Moat Cottage. To visit Nether Alderley Mill, continue along the lane to a junction with the A34 and turn left along this for 300 yards.

C. Nether Alderley Mill

The earliest mention of a mill here dates from 1290, but little is known about the building and no trace of the machinery survives. The present building is 16th century and was worked by a long line of millers until 1939 when declining trade and expensive repairs to dilapidated machinery forced it to close. The mill remained derelict and unusable until the 1950s when it was presented by the owner, Mr J A Shelmerdine, to the National Trust, which then set about restoring this historic gem to full working order.

The mill is constructed from warm red sandstone beneath a gritstone-flagged roof that almost reaches

Nether Alderley Mill

down to the ground on its front perspective. Inside there is a magnificent clutter of timber trusses, purlins, curved braces, wind braces and rafters, all made from oak and held together with wooden pins or 'trenails', just as the Elizabethan carpenters framed them up over 400 years ago. There is a superb atmosphere inside the mill and its complex arrangement of wheels, cogs, shafts and grinding stones is a joy to see in motion, especially when set against a background noise of creaking timbers, the click of cogs and the splashing of water from the two 'overshot' water-wheels that drive the machinery.

6 From here it is only a short step to visit the lovely church of St Mary's. To do this continue along the A34 for 70 yards then cross into a quiet lane, overhung by great beech trees and flanked by attractive cottages, with the church at its end.

D. St Mary's, Nether Alderley

This fine 14th-century church, built from warm pink sandstone contains many interesting features, including a Jacobean pew, situated over the south aisle and reached by steps from outside the church, used by the Stanley family, allowing them to worship away from the prying eyes of the riffraff below. In the churchyard stands the Old Schoolhouse, built in 1628 and used as such until 1908, together with a 19th-century extension which now serves as the village hall, and the Stanley family mausoleum. Together, these form one of the most attractive groups of sandstone buildings in the county.

7 After visiting, take the footpath on the far side of the church to reach the A34, cross and retrace your steps back to the stile opposite Moat Cottage. Climb the stile onto an enclosed footpath and at the end go left along the edge of a field to reach a ladder stile beside a gate leading onto a lane.

8 Go left along the lane to a stile on the right (100 yards before reaching the A34), then cross a field to a footpath running alongside a timber fence and past the rear of houses in Nether Alderley.

E. Nether Alderley

The history of this little village is dominated by the Stanley family, one of the oldest families in England and lords of the manor here for 500 years until 1938, when Lord Stanley was forced to relinquish it for sale in order to meet death duties. It is recorded in the Domesday survey as 'Aldredelie' and held by Godwin. The land, which was listed as consisting of arable land, meadowland,

Nether Alderley

woodland and several enclosures, was owned by Bigot de Loges.

The Stanley family seat was Old Hall, built in the 17th century, close to where the mill stands. It was destroyed by fire in 1779, rebuilt in the plain classical style, but destroyed by fire again in 1931; the building was then totally demolished.

9 At a junction with a broad lane turn right, past palatial houses, to join the drive leading to White Barn, but where the drive swings round to the right, continue ahead along a grassy swathe to climb a stile beside a gate. Proceed along a cinder path for 50 yards to a cross track, and go left along this to a bifurcation in front of an open meadow. Bear right here along the edge of woodland to join an enclosed footpath that climbs to reach the Macclesfield Road.

10 Cross onto a broad track leading to 'the Edge' and after 150 yards turn right alongside a fence to reach a magnificent viewpoint known as Castle Rock.

F. Alderley Edge

Castle Rock affords splendid views across Stockport, Manchester and beyond to the Pennine hills. Alderley Edge is a two-mile-long sandstone escarpment rising to an altitude of 625ft (190m). Prior to the 17th century and before the lord of the manor, Thomas Stanley, began to plant trees on the Edge, this massive sandstone outcrop was a desolate heath covered in gorse and heather. The National Trust acquired the Alderley Edge Estate in 1948 and now cares for 227 acres of woodland and some enclosed grazing pasture.

11 Continue along an undulating footpath running along the rim of the escarpment until opposite a wall corner over to the right then bear right and climb to the site of the Armada Beacon.

G. Ship Ahoy!

The Armada Beacon stood on the highest point of the Edge and was used as a lookout and to signal a warning of invasion from the Spanish Armada in 1588. There is no possible chance of viewing the sea from here, but it formed part of a chain of fire beacons that stretched the length and breadth of the country. It has been here since Tudor times but was unfortunately damaged (a photograph in the Wizard Information Centre dated 1929 shows evidence of structural damage) and demolished during a storm in 1931.

12 Numerous footpaths radiate out through this shady woodland but continue in roughly the same direction on a well-made footpath to reach the lip of the Engine Vein Mine.

H. Mining

The underlying rocks are rich in minerals, particularly copper and lead, and the whole area is riddled with pits, caverns and tunnels as a result of mining activities dating back to the Bronze Age. The mines have been worked intermittently until the early 20th century with three main mines in operation, the West Mine, the Wood Mine and this, the Engine Vein Mine. In the 20 years between 1857 and 1877, nearly 200,000 tonnes of copper ore were extracted from the mines.

For many years they were open to the public, but following several deaths and people getting lost in the labyrinth of passages, they were closed off. They have been excavated and surveyed by the Derbyshire Caving Club, and any member of the public wishing to visit this fascinating underground labyrinth can do so by contacting them.

13 Bear half right from the mine and follow the broad path through the trees to return to the Wizard car park.

I. Mystery and Legend

The name 'Wizard' stems from one of the many legends linked to this beauty spot. It refers to a wizard who, along with hundreds of sleeping warriors with white horses, occupies the underground caverns; they will all rise from their slumbers when England needs them.

Parking:	See Start and Finish
Public Transport:	None to the Wizard but service 130 Macclesfield – Manchester passes Nether Alderley Mill
Refreshments:	Wizard Inn and teashop at start of the walk
Tourist Information:	Small information office at the Wizard car park. Council Offices, Town Hall, Macclesfield SK10 1DX, Tel: 01625 504114
Nether Alderley Mill:	April, May and Oct: Wed, Sun and BH Monday 1–4.30; June – Sept: daily except Mon 1–5pm, Tel: 01625 523012
Hare Hill Gardens:	1 April – 30 Oct, daily except Mon, Tues and Fri (open BH Monday); 10 – 30 May daily 10–5.30pm, Tel: 01743 708100

WALK 7
Dunham Massey

*Altrincham – Dunham Park – Dunham
Massey – Little Bollington – Bridgewater Canal*

Distance:	6½ miles (10.4km)
Start and Finish:	Altrincham Station
Maps:	OS Explorer 268 (Wilmslow, Macclesfield and Congleton) and Explorer 276 (Bolton, Wigan and Warrington)

This is a walk of many contrasts that starts from the bustling centre of Altrincham, renowned throughout the area for its first-class transport system, superb market and excellent speciality shopping. The route then leaves suburbia for the tranquil countryside around Dunham Massey and Little Bollington. Dunham Massey Hall is set within 250 acres of parkland and is regarded by many as having Britain's most sumptuous Edwardian interiors, along with richly planted gardens. The return leg is along a lovely stretch of the Bridgewater Canal, the granddaddy of our canal network, being the first of its kind in England.

1 From the train and bus station walk past the Town Centre Clock, a historical feature of the town, and go left along Stamford New Road. Cross at the pedestrian lights and turn right into Shaws Road, which is largely traffic free, to reach a T-junction with Market Street and the market buildings to the left.

A. Altrincham
Altrincham is renowned as a historic market town, the original market charter being granted in 1290. Many of

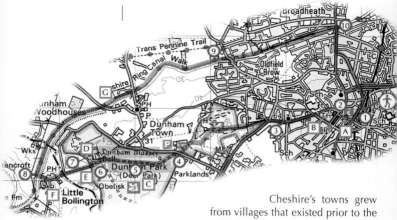

Cheshire's towns grew from villages that existed prior to the Norman Conquest but some, like Knutsford, were 'planted' – that is, they were new towns laid out on virgin sites. A number of people have suggested that the grid-like street pattern around Altrincham's market place may be a result of such a new town development, laid out after the granting of the market charter. Having established itself, the market thrived, a heritage that still holds true today with a splendid Market Hall that draws shoppers and visitors to almost 200 stalls that trade in everything from fish to frying pans and shoes to shallots.

2 Go left along Market Street, turning right at the end into Regent Road and follow this to a junction with the busy A56 Dunham Road. Cross the road via the footbridge on the right then head away from town along the A56, passing St Margaret's Church on the right with the Remembrance Gardens directly opposite.

B. Wealth in Abundance

This residential part of Altrincham was laid out after 1850 with opulent mansions set in extensive grounds and designed to cater for the town's men of wealth. During this part of the 19th century, the atmosphere and scenery around Altrincham were far more desirable than those of the industrial towns and cities. Added to this, there were good road and water links to Manchester, Liverpool, Warrington, Stockport and other major towns, complemented by the opening of the railway in 1849, when daily commuting became entirely feasible. Cotton magnates, property developers, architects, physicians and lawyers were all attracted here; in fact, by the end of the 19th century, this was the richest part of the county. Between 1800 and 1845, the town's population doubled to 6500, but after the coming of the railway in just 40 years it almost tripled this figure.

The Clock Tower, Altrincham

3 Cross Highgate Road, then Bradgate Road, where a gap in the chestnut fencing on the opposite side leads onto a track (signposted to Dunham Town) through Dunham Forest Golf and Country Club. This quiet track beneath the overhanging boughs of mature trees is quite a contrast to the stark exposure of the main road, and the roar of traffic soon gives way to the calls of songbirds and the occasional 'ping' as a well-aimed club strikes a golf ball. Lush fairways can be seen on either side through the trees, but just before the track leaves the shade of the trees in front of the 6th tee, bear diagonally left onto a narrow footpath which crosses a track after 40 yards. Continue through glades of trees before swinging left in front of the 12th tee onto a gravel footpath that runs alongside the tee. After 5 yards go left (footpath sign nailed to tree), and cross the end of a fairway (check the state of play before venturing across) to a continuation footpath running to the right of a car park before joining Charcoal Lane.

4 Go right for a few yards then cross to white-painted Charcoal Lodge Gates and a ladder stile leading into Dunham Park. (NB Dogs must be kept on leads at all times in the park.) Follow the broad, surfaced drive through the Deer Park, passing the elegant Deer Barn over to the right, and on towards the Hall.

C. The Deer Park

This extends to about 250 acres and is a rare survivor of an 18th-century formal design, with radial avenues lined with mature trees, created by George Booth, the second Earl of Warrington. Dunham Park is a fine example of a rare wildlife habitat called pasture-woodland, once a common form of land management around large country estates but now vanishing rapidly. Dunham Park is among the dozen most valuable sites of this type in the country and is a designated Site of Special Scientific Interest (SSSI).

A herd of some 200 fallow deer roams freely through the park with about 45 big bucks, distinguished by their large spreading antlers, and 70 breeding does with no antlers at all. There has probably been a herd here for over 500 years but it is thought that the Romans initially introduced this species to England almost 2000 years ago. Visitors are requested not to feed the deer.

5 The drive passes Smithy Pool on the right, a popular picnic spot, before swinging gently left in front of the hall.

D. Dunham Massey Hall

This dates back to Tudor times but was rebuilt by George Booth, the second Earl of Warrington, in the 1730s and extensively reworked in the early years of the 20th century. The result is an outstandingly beautiful mansion regarded by many as having the finest example of an Edwardian interior in these islands. There are exceptional collections of walnut furniture, books, silver and souvenirs of a grand tour of Europe. Over 30 rooms, each

Dunham Massey Hall

with its own unique atmosphere, are open to visitors in the house. The 10th Earl of Stanford, on his death in 1976, bequeathed the Dunham Estate – the hall, the park and over 3000 acres of land – to the National Trust.

Besides the house, the tranquil gardens with their flower- and shrub-filled borders, sweeping lawns and array of water features are well worth exploring. Remnants from past layouts are also visible, including an 18th-century orangery and the moat (now the lake), a reminder of the days when the site was occupied by a medieval castle.

Numerous events take place in the house and grounds throughout the season, including concerts, exhibitions, musical performances, dramatic productions, craft fairs and much, much more.

6 After visiting the hall and associated buildings, continue along the drive, passing to the left of the Old Mill and on towards Bollington gate where another ladder stile leads out of the park.

E. The Old Mill

With its mullioned windows, warm red brickwork, multi-gables, superb internal timberwork and stone-flagged floor, this building is a wonderful example of industrial architecture. It was originally built as a corn mill in 1616 but, with the building of the much larger Bollington Mill in the mid-19th century, it was converted to a saw mill. Little evidence survives today of the mill's original function, apart from the millstone dated 1684 – thought to be part of the original equipment – and a large iron ring bolted to a roof purlin, used to attach lifting gear for the sole purpose of changing or turning the millstones. A similar item can be seen in Nether Alderley Mill (see Walk 6).

By the mid-1800s it was redundant and started to fall into decay but has recently been restored to working order. Demonstrations are usually given on Wednesday and Sunday afternoons.

7 Once over the stile follow the broad, tree-lined avenue towards Little Bollington, crossing the little River Bollin with the splendid mill to the right. Pass the popular Swan with Two Nicks Inn (if you can!) then bear right along a cobbled lane with White Cottage to the right.

F. Little Bollington

White Cottage is the oldest property in the village and dates from about 1500. It was constructed as a cruck-trussed open hall with alterations in the 17th century. It has recently been restored by the National Trust using traditional materials and techniques and is now a private residence but can be visited thanks to the kind permission of the tenants (see Area Information).

Bollington Mill, Little Bollington

Once known as Bollington it was given the suffix 'Little' following government reorganisation in 1974 when the village became included in the same borough as 'Big' Bollington near Macclesfield.

The 'nicks' in the name of the inn refers to two small notches cut into the birds' bills in order that they could be identified to their owner, preventing them from being shot as wild birds. The superb four-storey mill is now a development of private apartments.

8 Once through the bridge beneath the Bridgewater Canal turn right up a flight of steps onto the towpath and turn left along this for a splendid 3 mile waterside walk.

G. The Granddaddy of Canals

The Bridgewater Canal was built in 1762 and was the first canal to be constructed entirely independent of any river system. It was designed to link the Duke of Bridgewater's collieries at Worsley with the Mersey at Runcorn, so avoiding the Mersey and Irwell Navigation and allowing the Duke's coal to be sent directly to

Old factories and mills line the Bridgewater Canal in Altrincham

Liverpool at a greatly reduced cost. It soon became an extremely busy waterway, not only for coal but also for heavy freight and agricultural produce. In the early 19th century the Bridgewater Canal packet shuttled back and forth along the canal, and on Sundays and Bank Holidays it would be filled with Mancunians seeking fresh country air here at Dunham Massey.

9 After 2 miles the Bay Malton Inn is passed at Oldfield Brow, after which the canal runs alongside old mills and factories that once relied heavily on waterborne transport for their livelihood.

10 Fifty yards beyond Altrincham Bridge, leave the towpath by turning left along a surfaced path into the car park of a shopping mall and go left through this to the A56. Turn left along this and over Altrincham Bridge, which was originally built in 1765, widened in 1830 and again in 1907, and eventually rebuilt to its present dimensions in 1935. Take the fourth road on the left, Barrington Road, and follow this back into town.

Parking:	Plentiful in Altrincham
Public Transport:	Trains from Manchester and Crewe, trams from Manchester, Tel: Metrolink 0161 205 2000; buses from many places, Tel: GMPTE 0161 242 6000
Refreshments:	All kinds in Altrincham; pubs at Little Bollington and Oldfield Brow; café at Dunham Massey
Tourist Information:	20 Stamford New Road, Altrincham WA14 1EJ, Tel: 0161 912 5931, Fax: 0161 941 7089
Dunham Massey:	National Trust, House: 27 March – 30 Sept, daily except Thurs and Fri 12–5pm (BH Sun and Mondays 11–5pm); Oct 12–4pm. Gardens: 27 March – 31 Oct daily 11–5pm, Tel: 01619 411025
White Cottage:	April – end Oct, last Sun of month 2–5pm. Visits must be booked through the Stamford Estate Office, Tel: 0161 928 0075

WALK 8
Gawsworth Hall

Bosley Top Lock – North Rode – Rodegreen –
Gawsworth Hall – Oakgrove – Macclesfield Canal

Distance:	6½ miles (10.5km)
Start and Finish:	Bosley Top Lock (grid ref: SJ904670)
Maps:	OS Explorer 268 (Wilmslow, Macclesfield and Congleton)

This walk of infinite variety through the parish of Gawsworth has all the ingredients for a fine day out. There are panoramic views over the foothills of the Peak District National Park, a beautiful section of the Macclesfield Canal, leafy lanes, grassy field paths, a chance to visit the splendid Gawsworth Hall and two fine pubs in which to take refreshment along the way.

Gawsworth Hall is a beautiful black and white half-timbered manor house dating back to the 15th century while the hamlet of Gawsworth contains several other fine buildings too, including the medieval church of St James, the Old Rectory and the New Hall, all of which are grouped around an attractive series of ancient fish ponds. The Macclesfield Canal is, once again, a lovely, used canal skirting the foot of the Pennine hills.

1 From the parking area beside bridge No 54 at Bosley Top Lock, turn right (west) along the lane to where it swings sharp right just beyond the railway bridge and here continue ahead along Park Road and along the drive to North Rode Manor. (If the gates are closed, climb the stile on the left.) The drive passes a large lake on the right, which usually has several species of waterfowl milling around, then

ascends round a bend to a cattle grid and gate. Turn left over a stile just before the cattle grid and cross the field towards the buildings of Yewtree Farm, then climb a stile at the right-hand side of the farm buildings to reach a surfaced farm drive in 30 yards.

The walk goes right here, along the drive, but it is well worth the short detour into the village of North Rode.

A. North Rode

North Rode is mentioned in the Domesday Book and used to be part of the parish of Prestbury until 1846 when it became a parish of its own. The church of St Michael was built in 1845 and consecrated on St John Baptist's Day, June 24th 1846. It is a handsome stone edifice with a square tower containing a large, single bell. Built in the Norman early English style, the church is gentle and graceful in

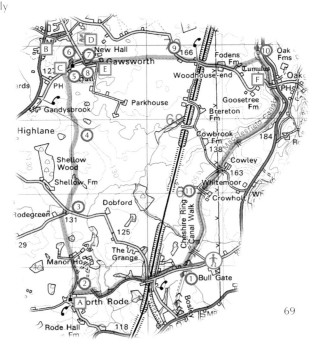

A tranquil Cheshire scene near North Rode

appearance. It consists of a nave, chancel and sanctuary paved with encaustic tiles, coloured using pigments mixed with hot wax which are then burned in as an inlay. The interior is warm and inviting with lovely carvings by local craftsmen and women and some colourful stained-glass windows in memory of members of the Dainty family who were the chief promoters and benefactors of the new church.

2 Turn right over the cattle grid and along the concrete drive leading to Manor Farm. At a fork in the track keep left to cross a second cattle grid beside farm buildings and continue ahead to a stile beside a gate. Cross a large, open field, heading towards buildings visible in Rodegreen; join a field track which runs round the left-hand side of a small wood on the far side of the field to a stile beside a gate. Continue along the left edge of a field to a stile, which leads onto a lane, and turn right along this past cottages in Rodegreen.

3 At the T-junction cross to climb a stile immediately left of the road signs, then walk along the left edge of the next two fields, cross a rough

track, and continue in the same direction through four more fields, first along the left edge then the right with the spire of Gawsworth church now directly ahead. This is a lovely scene, typical of this corner of Cheshire and one which has probably changed little over the centuries. Eventually the field-side footpath leads to a stile and track immediately in front of a series of ponds. Cross the track and stiles to the shore of the closest pond.

4 Turn left along the edge of the ponds, climb a short bank to a stile in the top left-hand corner of the field and walk along the left edge of the next three fields to reach a stile and steps leading down to a lane in the village of Gawsworth. The walk goes right here, but to visit the Harrington Arms, go left along the road for 250 yards.

B. Gawsworth

Situated on the eastern edge of the Cheshire plain, with some fine views towards the western fringes of the Peak District Hills, Gawsworth is a very beautiful, historic and peaceful village. It is highly likely that there has been a settlement here since Neolithic times, but it was recorded as 'Goursourde' in the Domesday survey and noted to be an area with extensive woodland and enclosures for oxen.

The cottages, farms, halls and church of the village blend with consummate ease into this soft landscape of broad, verdant fields and occasional copses. The Old Hall and church occupy the site of an early manor and wooden chapel that stood here when the De Orreby family owned the manor of Gawsworth back in the 1200s. Four of the five medieval fishponds still survive; the fifth one was situated in the low ground on the opposite side of the road to the church.

5 To continue the walk, turn right to reach a flight of steps on the right leading to the church of St James.

C. The Church of St James the Great

Built on the site of a Norman chapel, the 500-year-old roof and walls of the present church contain the magnificent tombs and special pews of four generations of the Fitton family, owners of the adjacent hall from 1316 to 1662. The oldest monument, situated to the right of the altar, is the table tomb that commemorates Francis Fitton, a knight who was buried at Gawsworth in 1608. This monument is made from freestone and alabaster and is the earliest example of Renaissance work in Cheshire. Another tomb belongs to Mary Fitton, Maid of Honour to Elizabeth I and possibly the Dark Lady referred to in William Shakespeare's sonnets:

'Shall I compare thee to a summer's day?
Thou art more lovely and more temperate . . .
So long as men can breathe or eyes can see,
So long lives this, and this gives life to thee.'
(Willliam Shakespeare, Sonnet XVIII)

The nave is the oldest part of the present church, built from limestone in 1430, followed by the magnificent 103ft-high tower constructed in 1480 from local pink sandstone.

6 From the church return to the road and go right, round the first of the medieval fish ponds and past the fine black and white building of the Old Rectory on the left, with New Hall directly ahead and Old Hall across the ponds to the right. This is a scene of utmost serenity and one which has probably changed little for centuries. Fine mature trees flank the ponds, ducks create ripples as they paddle back and forth, and the black and white timbers of the Old Hall are mirrored in the calm surface. All quintessential Cheshire.

D. New Hall

This is a fine and stately Georgian mansion built in the early 18th century by Lord Mohun. It was used as a

Gawsworth New Hall

Cheshire county home during the 20th century but is now privately owned. Lord Mohun was involved in what has been described as the most famous dual in British history, which took place in London in 1712. He was contesting the rightful inheritance of the Gawsworth Estates with the Duke of Hamilton, and the struggle involved forgery, corruption, seduction and even divorce. A dual took place between the two gentlemen in which both died, an event which considerably distressed Queen Anne, the last of the Stuart monarchs.

7 Where the road swings left in front of New Hall, turn right to reach the entrance to Gawsworth Hall.

E. Gawsworth Hall

The hall is privately owned and is a beautiful black and white half-timbered Tudor mansion picturesquely situated behind one of the medieval fishponds. The original Norman manor house, which once stood on the site, was rebuilt in 1480 by the Fitton family, but then extensively remodelled in 1701. It is steeped in history and it has been said that to see Cheshire, one must see Gawsworth.

As soon as you enter this charming home and walk

Gawsworth Hall

into the entrance hall, one is whisked back several hundred years; suits of armour, carved coats of arms, low ceilings and timber-framed walls bedecked with swords create a scene from medieval England. This is just a taste of what is to come as you tour this wonderful house which has been the setting for great events, intrigue and romance over the centuries. One of the most colourful characters to have lived at the hall was Samuel 'Maggoty' Johnson, England's last professional court jester who is buried in Maggoty Wood, just north of the hall.

The hall is now home to Timothy and Elizabeth Roper-Richards who open the building and its lovely gardens to the public during the summer months. A programme of musical and theatrical performances also takes place during the season, all to the fitting backdrop of this lovely old house.

8 From the hall turn right, passing cottages and a large statue of Robert Peel, and go along a lane skirting more ponds. Continue ahead to climb a stile beside a field gate with the tall, rectangular dwelling known as the Pigeon Tower over to the

left, and walk along the right edge of fields to emerge onto a lane near Mount Farm.

9 Turn right here, crossing the bridge over the railway and passing between roadside farm buildings to reach a track on the left with a footpath sign leading to Woodhouse Green Farm. Follow the track but once in the farmyard bear immediately right, pass through a gate then bear left, alongside farm buildings, to reach a pedestrian gate beside a field gate at the end of the buildings. Once over the stile bear right and descend this broad field, passing an isolated stile then an oak tree, to reach a stile and footbridge over a stream at the bottom of the field. Take the steps leading up to the towpath of the Macclesfield Canal.

10 Turn right along the towpath, passing through the hamlet of Oakgrove where those requiring refreshment will find the Fool's Nook Inn. This is a popular 18th-century pub with real character. It used to be called the Royal Oak,

The Macclesfield Canal near Oakgrove

but changed to the current name based on the fact
that the jesters from Gawsworth Hall used to meet
here. It has a cosy dining room with a warm,
cheery fire where home-cooked food using fresh
local produce ensures high quality at all times.

F. Macclesfield Canal

The construction work on the 27¾-mile-long canal began
in 1826 and was completed in 1831. It has 13 locks and
links the Peak Forest Canal at Marple to the Trent and
Mersey at Hardings Wood Junction and forms part of the
97-mile Cheshire Ring Canal Circuit. By the 1950s the
canal was little used, but thanks to an increased interest
in our waterways for pleasure purposes, this most attractive of canals running beneath the western fringes of the
Pennine hills was restored to full working order. On the
way along the canal, the view to the left is over
Gawsworth Common, the easternmost boundary of the
parish, which reaches an altitude of 1214ft (370m). It is
more typical of the high moorland scenery of the
Pennines than the undulating, hummocky country found
in the rest of the parish and creates a pleasing contrast.

11 Continue along the towpath for approximately 2 miles to return to Bosley Top Lock
and bridge No 54.

Parking:	See Start and Finish, otherwise park at Gawsworth or North Rode
Public Transport:	Service 201 Stagecoach Manchester; Manchester, Macclesfield, Leek runs along the 523, Tel: 01782 206608
Refreshments:	The Fool's Nook Inn, Oakgrove, and the Harrington Arms, Gawsworth
Tourist Information:	Council Offices, Town Hall, Macclesfield SK10 1DX, Tel: 01625 504114
Gawsworth Hall:	Privately owned, open April – Oct 2–5pm daily, Tel: 01260 223456 for all details

WALK 9

Jodrell Bank

Goostrey – Jodrell Bank – Kermincham Heath –
Swettenham – Kermincham Hall – Twemlow Green

Distance:	6¼ miles (11km)
Start and Finish:	Goostrey Station
Maps:	OS Explorer 268 (Wilmslow, Macclesfield and Congleton)

Cheshire has fine stately homes; it has evocative ruined castles; it has serene rivers, extensive canal networks and beautiful countryside, but at the beginning of the 21st century, Cheshire's most dominant and impressive landmark is Sir Bernard Lovell's radio telescope at Jodrell Bank. As we enjoy this pleasant walk in the shadow of the enormous telescope, just think of the wealth of knowledge it has provided since its completion in 1957 and whether it will still retain its dominant position as we head through another millennium.

Goostrey has its roots back in Saxon times and has one of the few remaining moated churches in the country. Jodrell Bank, along with its 35-acre arboretum, is an exciting place to study both nature and deep space, while Swettenham is one of the least changed villages in England with a lovely nature reserve, fine church and superb inn that has been acclaimed several times as Cheshire's pub of the year.

1 From the station turn right along the road towards Goostrey.

A. Goostrey and St Luke's Church
St Luke's Church, which dominates the eastern end of the village, is one of the few remaining churches in the

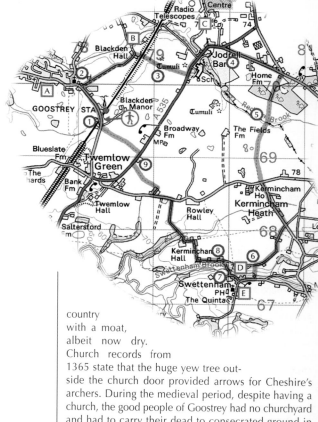

country
with a moat,
albeit now dry.
Church records from
1365 state that the huge yew tree outside the church door provided arrows for Cheshire's
archers. During the medieval period, despite having a
church, the good people of Goostrey had no churchyard
and had to carry their dead to consecrated ground in
Sandbach, eight miles away across marshy ground. In
1530 Goostrey's 'wakes walks' ended when the village
was granted a licence allowing them to bury their own
dead – providing they still paid their funeral dues to the
mother church in Sandbach!

Goostrey is mentioned in the Domesday Survey as
'Gostrel' in Middlewich Hundred with enough land for

one and a half ploughs. I have no idea how on earth you get on with only half a plough! One of the annual customs in the village is the showing of gooseberries and in order to compete you must be prepared for the judges to examine your berries during the growing season in order to prevent any monkey business.

2 Just beyond the village sign turn right onto a broad track with a footpath sign pointing to Jodrell Bank and Blackden Heath. The dishes and steel superstructures of the telescopes at Jodrell Bank, a familiar feature of the Cheshire landscape, soon come into view across the fields ahead. At Blackden Hall Farm walk past a barn on the right and follow the drive round to the left for a few yards before going right, inbetween farm buildings, into a rough area at the rear of barns. Turn right, following the footpath sign to Chelford Road; the rough track soon swings left then right beneath the railway line before running along the edge of fields.

B. Is There Anyone Out There?
The massive radio telescope dominates the skyline to the left at this point. The total structure weighs over 4700 tonnes, stands 292ft (89m) at its maximum height, has a dish diameter of 250ft (76m) and requires 9275 pints (5300 litres) of paint for three complete coats! The whole structure is fully steerable and is supported on two 180ft (55m) metal towers.

3 At the end of the track continue directly ahead to the end of the field; go right through a hedge gap then turn left along the edge of the next field to a junction with the A535. Cross with care onto a broad grassy verge on the opposite side and go left along this, past the entrance to Terra Nova School, to where the verge narrows. Proceed with great caution along the edge of the road into the hamlet of Jodrell Bank. Unfortunately it is not possible to

A winter view of Jodrell Bank from the Peak District hills

gain entrance to the radio telescope and arboretum from here, the public entrance being from Bomish Lane approximately 1½ miles to the north.

C. Jodrell Bank

For over 40 years the giant dish, known locally as Lovell's Saucer, has been quietly probing the depths of space in an attempt to unravel some of the mysteries of the universe. In order for it to keep its position among the giant telescopes of the world in the 21st century, extensive refurbishment is underway. On completion it will rank as one of the biggest and finest radio telescopes on Earth, giving us more information on pulsars, quasars, supernova, star clusters, gravitational lenses and who knows what other strange and exotic objects.

At the Jodrell Bank Science Centre there are excellent interactive exhibitions where you can discover for yourself the science of Earth, energy and space. Its planetarium is the largest outside London, with sophisticated projection and sound equipment which allows visitors to zoom in on the moon and stars, explore the planets and galaxies, and examine the mysterious nebulae.

Besides the aspects of space, you can also explore the Jodrell Bank nature experience and wander around the 35-acre arboretum which boasts over 2000 species of trees and shrubs.

A statue devoted to Copernicus, Jodrell Bank

4 Just beyond the entrance to Manchester University's School of Biological Sciences on the left, bear right into Farm Lane, a broad and quiet lane leading to Lower Withington. On the outskirts of the village pass the tiny corrugated building of St Peter's Church and, immediately beyond the car park of the Parish Hall on the right, go right along a track into woodland. At the other end of the wood climb a stile and bear slightly left across a broad meadow, climb another stile on the far side then descend a rough pasture towards trees where a footbridge spans Redlion Brook.

81

5 Once over, walk straight across another meadow heading for a stile beneath a lone oak tree in the far hedge and just right of a gate. Cross a farm track, often very muddy, then proceed along the left-hand side of two fields to a stile beside a gate and on alongside a fine avenue of oak trees before a stile leads onto a road. Cross into Congleton Road, turn right just beyond a row of houses at Kermincham Heath, past the entrance to Crosslane Farm, then 200 yards beyond the lovely buildings of Chestnut Farm go left over a stile into Swettenham Meadows Nature Reserve.

D. Swettenham Meadows Nature Reserve

This consists of 21 acres (8.5 hectares) of herb-rich grassland and flower meadows straddling Swettenham Brook. During the summer months a tangled web of flowers and grasses hums with bees and the air is filled with the dancing wings of comma, orange tip, small-, large- and green-veined white, peacock, tortoiseshell, wall and common blue butterflies. In winter a rich, earthy smell of rotting vegetation pervades, but the lack of leaves and cover makes it easier to spot the many wrens, robins, tits, redwings, thrushes and blackbirds which forage in the reserve, along with the electric blue of kingfishers that frequent the margins of the brook.

6 A narrow path zigzags down through the reserve to a footbridge over the brook followed by a short, steep ascent through a grassy meadow to a stile leading onto a lane. Turn right here into the village of Swettenham, bearing right alongside the parish church of St Peter towards the splendid Swettenham Arms, a fine inn that has received numerous accolades over the years, including *Cheshire Life* pub of the year.

E. Swettenham

Few villages can have changed so little over the centuries as Swettenham. Set in lovely countryside on the

The Swettenham Arms

north bank of the River Dane and cut off from the hustle and bustle of the outside world by a maze of narrow lanes, this quiet little backwater is one of Cheshire's many gems.

7 Take the footpath at the right-hand side of the pub car park, bear right alongside a rustic fence and past an attractive black and white half-timbered building to a junction with a track. Go right along this for 10 yards then turn left onto a broad track that descends to cross Swettenham Brook before climbing to Ashtree Farm.

8 Turn left along a track in front of the farm, and go through a farmyard onto a surfaced lane which you follow round to the right, by Brook Farm, and on to Deerpark Farm. Turn left here, then swing right just before the splendid buildings at Kermincham Hall, past a small pond on the right to eventually reach a junction with a road which is followed to the left for 300 yards. Immediately

beyond an attractive bungalow on the right, go right (footpath sign) along a broad track past barns, through a large gap in a hedge, then turn left alongside the hedge and through two fields to reach the busy A535.

9 Turn right along the road, then 75 yards past Blackyard Farm cross the road with care to a stile through a hedge; walk along the right side of a field to another stile and a footbridge in the far corner. Proceed along the left side of the next two fields, again with Lovell's radio telescope in view to the right, to a stile leading into a small copse of trees. Bear right along a narrow path that skirts the edge of a pond to join the drive leading to Blackden Manor and go left along this to the road which is followed the short distance back to Goostrey Station on the right.

Parking:	Goostrey village
Public Transport:	Trains from Crew, Stockport and Manchester; buses from Sandbach, Holmes Chapel, Knutsford and Altrincham, Tel: 01270 505350
Refreshments:	Pubs in Goostrey and Swettenham
Tourist Information:	20 High Street, Congleton CW12 1BD, Tel: 01260 271095

Jodrell Bank Science Centre and Arboretum:
Macclesfield, Cheshire SK11 9DL. Opening times vary, Tel: 01477 571339 (extension 4).

WALK 10

Little Moreton Hall

*Astbury – Macclesfield Canal – Ackers Crossing –
Little Moreton Hall – Brownlow Heath – Astbury*

Distance:	6½ miles (10.5km)
Start and Finish:	Astbury
Maps:	OS Explorer 268 (Wilmslow, Macclesfield and Congleton)

A historic village, quiet lanes, field- and canal-side foot-paths, broad vistas over Cheshire's green and pleasant land and a visit to one of the finest tim-ber-framed manor houses in all England make this a most enjoy-able and memorable walk. The going is always fairly easy with no ascents or descents of note.

Astbury is an attractive village with cottages grouped around the village green and domi-nated by the mas-sive church of St Mary's. The Macc-lesfield Canal is, once more, a busy waterway with numerous plea-sure craft either moored alongside or chugging along its length, and Little

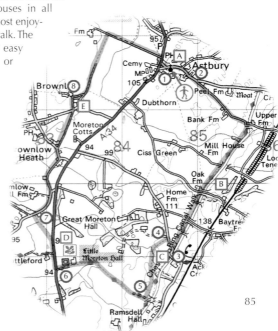

Moreton Hall must rank as one of the finest examples of a medieval black and white moated manor house in England.

1 From St Mary's Church turn right through the village and away from the A34.

A. Astbury

Astbury is a picturesque village with attractive cottages overlooking the village green, a friendly pub and a splendid church, the slim, recessed spire of which dominates the skyline for miles around. Despite its proximity to Congleton and the links with the textile industry, Astbury developed around agriculture and many of the houses in the village were built as estate workers' dwellings and not as weavers' cottages. The most striking feature of the village, however, is the splendid church of St Mary's, which towers over the village, dwarfing the surrounding cottages.

The castellated gateway to St Mary's, Astbury

2 At a fork in the road just beyond the village, go right along Dodd's Lane to reach the

Macclesfield Canal. Do not cross the bridge but descend steps on the left onto the canal towpath. Turn right beneath the bridge and follow this lovely canal-side footpath for 1¼ miles to the hamlet of Ackers Crossing.

B. Macclesfield Canal

This is just a small 27-mile contribution to Cheshire's 2000-mile canal network. Although never heavily industrialized, the county's desirable salt deposits and its geographical position between Liverpool, Manchester and the Midlands led to the building of the extensive canal network in the 18th and 19th centuries. The Macclesfield Canal links the Peak Forest Canal at Marple with the Trent and Mersey Canal at Kidsgrove in Staffordshire and passes through the old cotton and silk towns of Bollington, Macclesfield and Congleton on its lovely journey beneath the western fringes of the Pennine hills.

The Macclesfield Canal

3 Leave the towpath just before bridge No 85 by climbing steps onto New Road in Ackers Crossing. (**Do not continue beside the canal to bridge No 86 as there is no right of way from the towpath.**) Turn right, along the road, and round a sharp left-hand bend and alongside a small wood on the right. Just beyond the end of the wood climb a stile on the left, and next to the drive leading to Hall Farm, into a field.

4 Head straight across the field, passing between two electricity poles, to climb a stile immediately left of a small copse of trees on the far side. Bear slightly left across this next field, passing to the left of another electricity pole to reach a stile, then on past an isolated tree to a stile beside an iron field gate. Once over this, head straight down the next field to a stile leading onto a track, 75 yards right of canal bridge No 86.

C. Mow Cop

The ruins of the mock castle at Mow Cop are now visible on the hillside directly ahead. Built as a summer house by Randle Wilbraham in 1754, it was one of the first follies in England.

5 Go right, along the track, and over a stile beside a field gate then on beside the right-hand hedge of this and the next field. At the end of the second field climb a stile and bear left towards Little Moreton Hall Farm, crossing the farm track before passing to the left of the farm buildings and onto the entrance drive to Little Moreton Hall.

D. Little Moreton Hall

Little Moreton Hall is an absolute joy in every possible way, a fact borne out by the number of books, booklets, magazines and calendars that feature this wonderful black and white timber-framed manor house. Almost entirely medieval in style, and little changed over the years, it exudes history with its overhanging gables, distorted timbering, gallery windows and secret rooms. On a calm day the surrounding moat creates a perfect mirror image of the hall; the only things to break the reflection are the ripples from rising fish and bow waves from the resident ducks.

6 After visiting the hall walk along the drive and past the car park to cross the busy A34 before turning right along the footpath. Luckily, the walk only follows the road for 500 yards after which a

stile by a footpath sign leads into a field (a short distance past the entrance to Cuttleford Farm). Proceed alongside the left field hedge initially then continue forward, across the open field, heading to the left of a dwelling visible ahead. On the far side of the field, pass through the left of two hedge gaps and walk alongside a drainage ditch and hedge on the right to reach a lane.

7 Turn right along the lane, past the entrance to Alcumlow Hall Farm, then as the road forks keep left to reach a T-junction. Turn left past Ivy Cottage, continuing towards the houses at Brownlow Heath but turn right by a bridleway sign immediately in front of the houses and along a tarmac lane. After a short distance join a sandy footpath between trees, cross a lane after 300 yards, then bear slightly left onto a continuation track leading towards Brownlow Farm. Just beyond the entrance to the farm, turn right by a footpath sign and walk along a broad, grassy, hedged-in track.

Little Moreton Hall

Out for a stroll near Brownlow Heath

E. Steeple Views

The shapely steeple of St Mary's Church in Astbury is now clearly visible directly ahead. A unique feature of the tower is that it stands isolated from the nave, suggesting that it was built before the church, possibly in the late 1200s.

8 The track descends at first before swinging gently leftwards (ignore a track to the right) to enter a field where the right field edge is followed through this and other fields to reach a concrete farm drive. Turn right along the drive, which joins the A34 on the outskirts of Astbury.

Parking:	Limited near the church in Astbury
Public Transport:	Cheshire County Council Service 77 Congleton – Hanley and Service 315 Congleton – Rode Heath; not Sundays, Tel: 01270 505350
Refreshments:	Pub at Astbury; café at Little Moreton Hall
Tourist Information:	Town Hall, High Street, Congleton CW12 1BN, Tel: 01260 271095
Little Moreton Hall:	National Trust, open 21 March – 1 Nov: daily except Mon and Tues 12–5.30pm (open BH Mondays); 7 Nov – 20 Dec: Sat and Sun 12–4pm, Tel: 01260 272018

WALK 11

Lyme Park and Hall

*Disley – Cage Hill – Lyme Hall – West Parkgate –
Bakestonedale Moor – Bow Stones – East Lodge*

Distance: 8¼ miles (13km)

Start and Finish: Disley

Maps: OS Outdoor Leisure 1 (The Peak
District, Dark Peak area)

In 1397 Peter Legh was granted land at Lyme Handley,
part of the Royal Forest of Macclesfield and famous for
its large herds of red deer, as a reward for contributions
made by the family during campaigns in France. This
was the start of a long-lasting relationship, with the
estate passing from father to son, grandfather to grandson until 1946 when Richard Legh donated Lyme to the
National Trust. This superb walk through the grounds of

*The square and war
memorial at the start
of the walk, Disley*

91

Lyme Park gives a magical blend of history, nature and splendid scenery.

Disley is a busy little town on the A6, perched on the borders between Derbyshire and Cheshire. The Cage is a hunting tower, recently restored, although Lyme Hall was transformed by the Italian architect Leoni into one of the most sumptuous and biggest houses in Cheshire, and the surrounding park land supports a large herd of red deer. The Bow Stones are believed to be parts of ancient Saxon crosses.

1 From the war memorial in the centre of Disley walk past the Ram's Head Inn towards Higher Disley but, immediately beyond the pub, bear right

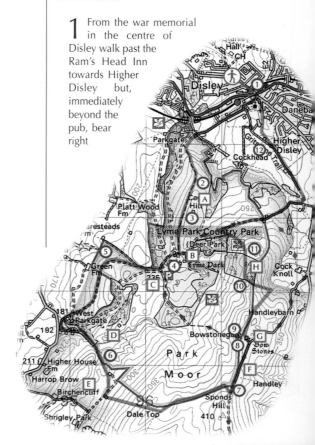

into Red Lane. This quiet lane leads past the entrance to the church of St Mary the Virgin then swings round to the right, past fine houses on the outskirts of Disley and on to a gate leading into the grounds of Lyme Park. Continue ahead towards a kiosk and the main entrance drive and turn left along this for approximately 200 yards to a stand of mature, mixed woodland set astride the drive and bear left here along a rough track that climbs onto the slopes of Cage Hill.

The Cage

2 At a Y-fork just beyond the depressions left from old coal measure workings, bear left towards the Cage which has recently been restored and is now open to the public.

A. The Cage

Some form of tower has stood here since 1524 but the present building was the work of Leoni in the 1730s. The original purpose would have been a hunting tower from which the ladies of the house could view the progress of the gentlemen as they hunted in the park. It became known as the Cage in the 17th century when it took on the slightly more gruesome role as a prison for folk caught poaching in the park. They were 'caged' in one of the small rooms in the tower until they could be taken for trial in Macclesfield.

3 Continue past the Cage, following the broad track along the brow of Cage Hill which leads

93

towards the stylish building of Lyme Hall. Cross the drive then bear right just before the main gates and descend steps into the car park.

B. Lyme Hall

The earliest house here would most probably have been a modest lodge – a record from about 1200 describes the dwelling as 'one fair hall with its high chamber', used as an overnight shelter whilst hunting. By 1465 the Leghs had decided to build something more substantial.

In 1570 the whole house was totally remodelled by Peter Legh VII; the present east and north sides of the house were part of this reconstruction along with the magnificent porch leading into the courtyard. Minor improvements and modifications were made over the next 200 years, but it was in the late 17th century that radical alterations were made, leaving the hall much as we see it today. Peter Legh X employed the talents of the Venetian architect Giacomo Leoni, who transformed Lyme into an Italianate palace and one of the largest houses in Cheshire.

Lyme beamed its way into the homes of millions in the UK during 1995–6 when it starred as the exterior of Pemberley in the BBC adaptation of Jane Austen's novel

Lyme Hall

Pride and Prejudice. Since then the visitor figures to Lyme have zoomed by 250% and a special Pemberley Trail has had to be introduced in order to stop visitors stumbling into neighbouring gardens in search of the lake that our attractive Mr Darcy swam across! I don't know what they expect to see when they find it, Mr Darcy's pride still reflecting in the waters perhaps? Or am I being prejudiced!

4 Cross the car park onto the West Drive and walk up to a fork at the brow of a hill. Take the right-hand branch for a short distance to another fork but this time go left along a track skirting the Knott, a rounded hillock which is a favourite with children as a spot for kite flying and games of roly-poly. After passing through a gate, continue ahead with the urban sprawl of Manchester and Stockport forming the skyline. The track soon swings left to reach a wooden kissing gate through a tall deer fence which also forms a boundary fence to the park.

C. Red Deer

Lyme has a large herd of red deer which roam freely throughout the park. The Legh family originally came to Lyme for the deer, providing sport for themselves and numerous illustrious visitors like James Duke of York, later King James II. The red deer of Lyme were so important to the Leghs that their family crest incorporates the head of a fine 14-pronged stag.

5 The path follows a lush, grassy track through a large open pasture to a gate and ladder stile at the far end. On the far side go left along the drive leading to Green Farm, past the West Parkgate entrance to Lyme, to a junction with Shrigley Road near a little Methodist chapel. Turn left, then left again along a track at the side of the chapel leading to Green Close Farm. The track rises steadily past cottages at first but at the top of the rise you must pass through a gate and over a stile into a field

*The moors above
Lyme Park*

and walk along its left edge, with the wooded slopes of Cluse Hay falling away to the left.

D. Wild Moorland

The walk now changes its character as it heads out into wild, open moorland with the call of the curlew and song of the skylark for company.

6 The path heads to the right after a while, avoiding a wooded dell, before rising steadily towards Bakestonedale Moor with the buildings of Moorside ahead. Pass to the right of Moorside on a made-up path across a rather boggy section of moor to a stile leading onto a track. Turn right along the track then left immediately beyond Keeper's Cottage (footpath sign to Browstonegate and Kettleshulme) and follow the gently rising footpath alongside the drystone wall towards Dale Top and the western slopes of Sponds Hill.

E. Seven Counties

On a clear day it is possible to see seven counties along with the Clwydian hills from the top of Sponds Hill; it may well be worth the short detour to the top.

7 At the top of the rise climb a stile and head left along the wallside footpath towards the white-painted buildings at Brownstonegate.

F. Bell Pits

The shallow depressions in the moor just beyond the stile are the remains of old coal pits.

8 The path eventually runs along a walled-in track to reach a lane end where, on the opposite side of the road in a small fenced-in enclosure, the Bow Stones are situated.

G. Bow Stones

The Bow Stones are believed to be the middle sections of Saxon crosses, probably placed here to mark some ancient boundary. One of the cross heads now resides in the Legh family chapel at Lyme Hall.

9 The walk continues left over a stile beside the farm drive, following the footpath sign to Lyme Park. At the far side of the field climb a ladder stile beside a wooden gate to re-enter Lyme Park. However, you must turn right, off the main path which is part of the Gritstone Trail, and follow the wallside footpath, passing a memorial pictogram indicating places and distances visible from this point. At a junction with a cross-wall turn left and descend alongside Lantern Wood to a wooden ladder-stile leading over the wall on the right and into the wood.

10 The broad track through the wood adds yet another variant to this walk of contrasts, and on warm, still days the fragrant aroma of pine is very distinct as the resin slowly distills into the Cheshire air. Halfway through the wood the folly known as the Lantern is passed in a clearing on the left.

H. The Lantern

The Lantern is one of the more curious features in the park, and is so called due to its similarity to an old-fashioned lantern. It originally adorned the top of the Elizabethan hall, but the architect Leoni thought it rather incongruous with the rest of his completed design so had it removed and erected on a new base in Lantern Wood.

11 At the far side of the wood climb a stile and head across a short section of pasture to reach a drive and go right along this to East Lodge. Pass through the gates beside the Lodge and follow a broad track over Bollinghurst Brook and on to a junction with another track by a footpath sign. Go left here, following the sign pointing to Green Lane, which bears left just beyond the enclosed copse to reach a gate leading onto an enclosed footpath which eventually becomes a broad track.

12 At Stoneridge Farm turn right into the farmyard and go through a gate immediately alongside the farm building. Bear right across two fields. Climb a stile in the far corner of the second field, continue past new houses to a T-junction with another footpath and go left down steps to a road with the old Quaker Meeting House to the left. Go right back into Disley.

Parking:	Large car park between Ram's Head Inn and Disley station
Public Transport:	A number of services run through Disley, Tel: 0161 228 7811; trains to Disley from Manchester and Stockport, Tel: 08459 484950
Refreshments:	Pubs and cafés in Disley; tea room at Lyme Hall (when open); café at Park Shop, open Nov–March 2000 Sat and Sun 12–4pm.
Tourist Information:	Graylaw House, Chestergate, Stockport SK1 1NG, Tel: 0161 474 3320
Lyme Park:	For opening times and events Tel: 01663 766492, E-mail: lymepark@nationaltrust.org.uk

WALK 12
Capesthorne Hall

*Redes Mere – All Saints Church,
Siddington – Northwood Farm – Crabtree Moss
Farm – Henbury Moss – Capesthorne Hall – Redes Mere*

Distance:	8½ miles (13.7km)
Start and Finish:	Car park at southern end of Redes Mere (grid ref: SJ848713)
Map:	OS Explorer 268 (Wilmslow, Macclesfield and Congleton)

This is a fairly long but easy walk through the fertile farmland of this part of the county. Grassy meadows, quiet woodland, ponds and meres rich in wildfowl, a beautiful church and the chance to visit the splendid Jacobean-style Capesthorne Hall make for a most enjoyable day out.

All Saints Church at Siddington is a truly beautiful, partly-timbered building with a warm, quiet and peaceful interior. Capesthorne Hall with its towers and turrets, set in over 100 acres of picturesque parkland, is quite unique among the county's stately homes, while the shallow waters of Redes Mere and the lakes at Capesthorne are excellent venues for numerous species of waterfowl.

1 From the car park go left (west) along Fanshawe Lane and past the southern tip of Redes Mere.

A. Redes Mere
This is an artificial lake, held back by a small dam built across Fanshawe Brook at the northern end of the mere. It is a popular place for families who come to feed the flocks of waterfowl, which include amongst their numbers tufted duck, great crested grebe, ruddy duck, mallard, pochard, mute swans, canada geese, golden eye, coot, moorhens

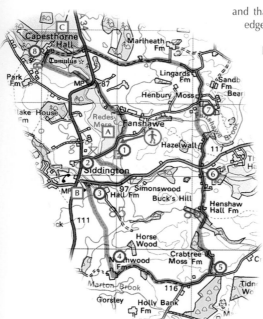

and that most astute of water's-edge prowlers, the grey heron. The mere is fairly shallow and when the water is particularly low, strange clumps of dead vegetation become exposed. These floating islands were described and enhanced by Alan Garner in his children's novel *The Weirdstone of Brisingamen*.

2 Seventy-five yards beyond the mere go left over a stile by a public footpath sign, walk along the right edge of a field to another stile, then bear diagonally left through a sloping meadow to a stile through the far hedge. Proceed in the same direction over the brow of the next meadow to reach a stile beside a gate leading onto the B5392. Turn right along this but, 50 yards before a junction with the A34, go sharp left along the access drive to All Saints Church.

B. All Saints Church, Siddington

This is a fascinating old church, mellowing amidst lush, verdant pastures overlooked by the foothills of the Pennines. Records from various sources mention the presence of a chapel at Siddington in 1337 and also in 1474, but the present building was not consecrated until 1521. In 1721 it was licensed for baptisms, marriages and to 'bury in ye chapel yard but not in ye chapel'; prior to this most of these services had taken place in the mother church, St Peter's in Prestbury.

It was originally a completely timber-framed chapel, but in 1815 the outer walls were clad in brick in order to support the heavy Kerridge flag-stone roof which was causing the walls to bulge. Beneath the bricks, some of which have been painted to mimic the original half-timbered structure, is the original frame of the building, most of which can still be seen when you enter this warm, peaceful and tranquil church which has been a place of worship for over 700 years.

The attractive little bell turret houses a single tenor bell cast in 1588 which was intended to be rung to warn parishioners of the impending Spanish invasion. Instead it peeled across the fields in celebration of the defeat of the Armada.

3 Pass through a gate at the far end of the churchyard, head across a field to another gate and, once through, bear slightly right through the adjacent field to the far fence and a stile, which is partly obscured by a holly bush. Cross the

Redes Mere

next two meadows, now with views of the Peak District hills to the left and the rather prominent shapely outline of Shining Tor. In the third meadow bear slightly right, heading away from the fence line to a stile at the bottom. Now bear diagonally right through a narrow field, climb the right-hand stile and walk up the left side of a very large pasture, heading towards the buildings at Northwood Farm.

4 Seventy-five yards before the farm, go left over a stile signposted to Crabtree Moss. Walk round the right edge of a field to reach a surfaced farm track and turn left and follow this all the way to Morton Lane. Go left along the lane to reach the access drive to Crabtree Moss Farm on the left.

5 Walk along the drive to a Y-fork just in front of the farm, bear right for 30 yards then veer left between farm buildings to reach a gate leading into a field. Bear slightly left at first, joining a rough field track with Moss Wood to the left. Stay on the track as it swings right through the next field, then descend into Heskey Wood before reaching Henshaw Hall Farm. Pass to the left of the buildings and through the farmyard, then follow the access drive out to the B5392.

6 Cross to a stony track on the opposite side, pass houses at Hazelwall, climb a stile at the far end of the track and circumnavigate trees and shrubs on the right to reach a stile over a fence. Head straight across the next field, cross a footbridge spanning Fanshawe Brook and negotiate a boggy section of woodland before walking up the left edge of a field to reach Fanshawe Lane.

7 Go right along this to reach Lingards Farm and turn left immediately beyond the buildings

Capesthorne Hall

and through the farmyard, proceed along the right edge of two fields to reach a stony track and follow this out to reach the A34, directly opposite the East Lodge entrance to Capesthorne Hall. To visit the hall cross the road and walk along the drive for quarter of a mile. Otherwise, to continue turn left along the A34 and rejoin the walk at point 8.

C. Capesthorne Hall

With its towers, turrets and distinctive Jacobean façade, Capesthorne Hall is quite unique amongst Cheshire's stately homes. Set in 100 acres of glorious parkland, Capesthorne has been touched by nearly 1000 years of English history. Roman legions marched across its acres; Norman nobility hunted in the great forests that once carpeted the region, and during the English Civil War a Royalist ancestress helped Charles II to escape after the Battle of Worcester.

The oldest part of the present house dates from the Georgian period but this was considerably altered by the architect Edward Blore in 1834. A disastrous fire in 1861 destroyed much of the hall so the famous architect

Anthony Salvin was employed to build a new central portion in the Jacobean style.

Capesthorne is mentioned in the Domesday Book as 'Copestor' in the Macclesfield Hundred. In 1153 the Davenport family were appointed custodians of the Royal Forest of Macclesfield and the family have governed the estate ever since; the present squire is William Bromley Davenport, Lord Lieutenant of Cheshire. The crest of the Davenport family is a rather gruesome motif that dates from the Norman period and depicts a falcon's head in a hangman's noose, a symbol of the position and power that the family held in the Middle Ages – the power to control life and death.

The hall contains collections of fine art, marble sculptures, furniture, tapestries and antiques from Europe, America and the Far East. The gardens are quite splendid and the grounds slope down to a chain of attractive lakes which are spanned by a graceful, multi-arched bridge.

8 After visiting the hall and grounds, walk down to the lakes, cross the bridge and immediately turn left along a field and past a wood to reach the A34. Cross over the road with care to a track on the far side and follow this alongside Redes Mere and past the Sailing Club. Keep along a lakeside footpath that eventually leads out to Fanshawe Lane and the car park.

Parking:	See Start and Finish
Public Transport:	Arriva service 75, Congleton – Macclesfield, passes through Siddington
Refreshments:	Café/restaurant at Capesthorne Hall
Tourist Information:	Council Offices, Town Hall, Macclesfield SK10 1DX, Tel: 01625 504114; 20 High Street, Congleton CW12 1BD, Tel: 01260 271095.
Capesthorne Hall:	Open April – Oct, Weds, Suns and BH Mondays; for information Tel: 01625 861221

WALK 13

Marple

Marple Station – Peak Forest Canal – Kirk Wood – Chadkirk – Middlewood Way – Macclesfield Canal

Distance:	5½ miles (8km)
Start and Finish:	Marple Station, Station Road
Map:	OS Outdoor Leisure 1 (The Peak District Dark Peak area)

The towpaths of the Macclesfield and Peak Forest Canal, along with the leafy glades of the Middlewood Way, are favourite jaunts for local residents in Marple but few outside the area know of the wealth of industrial archaeology here. This lovely walk takes in sections of both canals and part of the Way, along with some of the surrounding countryside to the north, west and south of the town.

The Peak Forest Canal lifts boats through 209ft between a flight of 16 locks in Marple. Benjamin Outram's fine aqueduct took seven years to build, is 309ft long and rises some 100ft above the River Goyt. Chadkirk is an ancient manor mentioned in the Domesday Book, while Chadkirk Chapel has associations with the seventh-century missionary St Chad. Marple and its close neighbour Mellor owe much of their development to one agricultural and industrial entrepreneur, Samuel Oldknow.

1 From the railway station go right onto the A626 but just before the canal bridge, on the outskirts of Marple, turn right onto the towpath.

A. Peak Forest Canal

This section of the Peak Forest Canal was completed in 1805 and replaced a tramway that connected two sections of the waterway. The tramway, an inclined plateway, was a

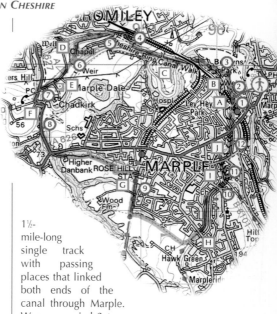

1½-mile-long single track with passing places that linked both ends of the canal through Marple. Wagons carried 2 tonnes each along the 4ft 2in-gauge track and were lowered under gravity. On busy days over 600 tonnes of cargo were handled and nightwork was introduced to cope with the heavy traffic.

2 Walk along the towpath passing Locks 8 to 1, along with their canal ponds, which store water and reduce water loss down the overflow culverts.

B. Wildlife

Swan, mallard, coot and moorhen are common along this stretch of the canal and at quiet times you may spot a heron, majestically poised along the towpath. Around Lock 4, the bank is covered with butterbur, the large, fleshy leaves of which were used for wrapping butter, hence the name.

3 Just beyond Lock 1 and alongside Aqueduct House, once a busy blacksmith's and carpenter's shop, cross the canal via Bridge 16 before continuing along the towpath on the opposite side. The canal now passes beneath the railway bridge before crossing the magnificent Marple Aqueduct.

C. Marple Aqueduct

Designed by Benjamin Outram, the overall engineer for the Peak Forest Canal, this majestic three-arched structure is 309ft long and carries boats some 100ft above the dark waters of the River Goyt below. It took seven years to build and was opened in 1800. Shortly after crossing the aqueduct the canal runs through a narrow cutting, the remains of the old Rose Hill Tunnel which collapsed over 100 years ago. The Peak Forest Canal Company was set up on March 28th 1794, and two months later an Act of Parliament allowed building work to start. Three distinct operations began simultaneously – construction of this lower canal from bottom Lock 1 to Ashton-under-Lyme; construction of the upper section of the canal from top Lock 16 to Buxworth near Whaley Bridge; and the building of the tramway between the two ends through Marple.

The towpaths of the Peak Forest Canal are a popular jaunt for locals

The aqueduct and railway viaduct spanning the Goyt Valley

4 On reaching the 1104ft long Hyde Bank Tunnel, it is necessary to leave the canal because there is no towpath through it. At this point the horses would be unhitched and taken over ground, while the bargeman would leg the boat through the tunnel by lying on his back across the barge and literally walking along the walls of the tunnel. At a junction with a track go left past Hyde Bank Farm, follow this round to the left, then bear left along a footpath signposted to Valley Way, which passes beneath a low stone bridge before rejoining the towpath.

5 Continue alongside the canal for a further 100 yards, until just before factory units on the opposite side, then go left along a footpath signposted 'Midshires Way' that runs along the left edge of Kirk Wood.

D. Ancient Woodland

Much of the woodland here is ancient woodland, which means that it was established before 1600. Native species like oak, ash, holly and hawthorne are present along with introduced species such as sycamore and beech. In total there are 19 species of tree in this area, including four species of oak. The fauna and flora beneath the trees are also most interesting, with over 60 species of plant being identified, and because of this Greater Manchester Countryside Unit have designated the area a grade 'A' Site of Biological Importance.

6 The path eventually descends a flight of broad steps to a T-junction with another footpath. To visit the little Chadkirk Chapel turn right, but to continue the walk turn left to a junction with Vale Road and follow this out to a junction with the A627 at Chadkirk.

E. Chadkirk

Unlike Marple, the ancient manor of Chadkirk found its way into the Domesday Book where it was described as being some 3 miles long by 1½ wide and as having a value of 10 shillings. Inflation has probably made it worth a few bob more today! Although legend has it that the manor has associations with the seventh century missionary St Chad, the little chapel only dates from the early 16th century. It is open during weekends, 1–5pm, and has an informative audiovisual show giving the history of the building and the life of St Chad.

7 Turn left along the A627 which soon swings left over the River Goyt via Otterspool Bridge.

F. River Goyt

The river is certainly more tranquil than the road, but it must be a long time since the elusive creatures that gave the bridge its name frolicked in the waters below.

8 Continue along Dooley Lane, passing Wyevale Garden Centre (which has a café) on the left and the Hare and Hounds Tavern on the right, to eventually reach a junction with the Stockport Road. Cross with care onto a narrow lane on the opposite side, which leads to Higher Danbank

Farm. Keep left at a Y-fork and left of all the farm buildings to join a rough track running along the edge of the fields. Where the track enters a field, keep left along the edge of the wood to the far fence, go right along this to a stile on the left and once over walk along the right side of a meadow, joining an enclosed track on the far side that leads to a bridge spanning the old railway line. Once over, turn right, down steps onto the old track bed and go left along this.

G. Middlewood Way

This is the Middlewood Way, a former railway line converted by Stockport and Macclesfield Borough Councils into an attractive linear park. It runs for 11 miles from

The Middlewood Way

Marple to Macclesfield and provides a pleasant, vehicle-free route for walkers, cyclists and horse riders.

9 After 200 yards, cross a parking area and lane to rejoin the way. Continue for a further 300 yards then go left at a cross-path, climbing a stile (footpath sign to Macclesfield Canal) into the grounds of Marple Golf Club. Walk along the left edge of the course initially, then along the top of a wood before eventually crossing open fairways (waymarkers) to reach the towpath of the Macclesfield Canal and turn left along this, passing the massive Goyt Mill on the opposite bank.

H. Goyt Mill
Built in 1905 and closed in 1960, this fine building may well vie for the title of the most southerly cotton mill to be built in England; only silk mills were south of here. The mill is now divided up into small factory units.

10 At Bridge No 2 cross the canal to rejoin the towpath on the opposite side, but if refreshment is required, the Ring O' Bells Inn on the right of the bridge is highly recommended.

I. Carpenter's Shop
Just beyond the bridge on the opposite side of the canal is the old Carpenter's Shop with its shipping hole entrance leading to a covered waterway. The heavy wooden lock gates were constructed in here and then lowered directly into the barges parked in the covered waterway.

11 Bridge No 1, situated at the junction with the Peak Forest Canal, is known as a roving bridge because it allowed horses to change tow-paths without having to be uncoupled from the boat. There are fine views eastward from the parapet of the bridge over Marple Marina to Mellor church, framed by the huge bulk of Kinder Scout beyond. Once over the bridge descend alongside

The old Carpenter's Shop on the Macclesfield Canal

the splendid flight of locks, and their large canal ponds, through Marple.

J. Marple Locks

These not only acted as water catchment ponds but also allowed boats to queue while navigating the locks or wait their turn to enter the lime-loading sheds at Marple Lime Kilns, just beyond the ponds. This flight of 16 locks, built in two years and opened in 1805, raises the canal 210ft and, at an average of 13ft, they are much deeper than those normally engineered.

12 Pass beneath Posset Bridge, using the narrow horse tunnel (notice the narrow passage and steps on the right used by the boatmen), proceed past Oldknow's Warehouse on the right, now converted into offices but still preserving the shipping hole entrance at the front, to reach Station Road. Turn right along this back to Marple Station.

Parking:	Opposite Marple Station or otherwise plentiful in Marple
Public Transport:	Trains from Manchester Piccadilly and Sheffield, Tel: 08459 484950; buses from Manchester, Stockport, Disley and New Mills, Tel: 0161 273 3300
Refreshments:	All types in Marple; pub at Chadkirk
Tourist Information:	Graylaw House, Chestergate, Stockport SK1 1WG, Tel: 0161 474 3320

WALK 14
Northwich

*Northwich – Weaver Navigation – Marston –
Trent and Mersey Canal – Anderton – Winnington*

Distance:	7½ miles (12km)
Start and Finish:	Town Bridge, Northwich
Map:	OS Explorer 267 (Northwich and Delamere Forest)

The area around Northwich offers a splendid opportunity to explore the region's industrial heritage and gain a fascinating insight into that most important of commodities – salt. This virtually flat walk explores canals, navigations, salt works, ingenious boat lifts, Edwardian pumping stations and museums, and even passes the site of the last battle of the English Civil War.

The Salt Museum in Northwich gives a fascinating insight into an ancient industry that has brought prosperity

*Town Bridge and
the start of the walk*

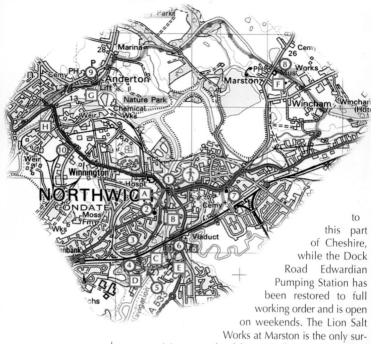

to this part of Cheshire, while the Dock Road Edwardian Pumping Station has been restored to full working order and is open on weekends. The Lion Salt Works at Marston is the only surviving example of the original open-pan method of salt extraction, and Anderton Boat Lift is an extraordinary example of Victorian ingenuity and engineering.

1 From Town Bridge follow the towpath alongside the River Weaver southwards towards Hayhurst Bridge.

A. First in Britain

Hayhurst and Town Bridge, built in 1898 and 1899 respectively, are believed to be the first electrically powered swing bridges in Britain and the first to be built on floating pontoons. Both of these initiatives came about because of subsidence due to salt extraction; electric cables, unlike pipes, bend rather than break when the ground gives way and a floating pivot is totally unaffected by subsidence. The idea of building two bridges also meant that road traffic could always enter or leave the town when one or other structure was swung open to allow a ship to pass.

2 At Hayhurst Bridge cross Chester Way, bear right for a few yards on the opposite side and then go left along Navigation Road, passing the navigation offices on the left, now the regional offices of British Waterways.

B. Clock Tower

The attractive Georgian clock tower was built in 1830, four years after the main building; both are now Grade II listed buildings. A little further along the road is Navigation House, also a Grade II listed building, dating from around 1856 and constructed as a home, office and stables for the engineer-in-charge of the Weaver Navigation Trust.

3 Continue on along Spencer Street to the end of a new brick wall surrounding a modern housing development on the left and turn left along an enclosed footpath that passes beneath the railway viaduct.

C. Railway Viaduct

This impressive structure, built in the early 1860s, is over 1000 yards long (900m) and consists of 48 arches and two iron-girder spans. It crosses three water courses: the River Dane, the old course of the River Weaver and the Weaver Navigation.

4 At a junction with a surfaced footpath go left to reach the Weaver Navigation at Hunt's Locks.

D. Weaver Navigation

Northwich was already the market leader in Cheshire by the late 17th century, but when the River Weaver was

The magnificent railway viaduct and Hunt's Locks, Northwich

improved by creating the Weaver Navigation in the 1720s and 30s, the town's prosperity boomed. It meant that Lancashire coal could now be easily brought in and salt shipped out in ever increasing loads. Pack-horses had been the main form of transport until then, each carrying a load of 200lbs, but with the coming of the navigation, 100 ton loads could be conveyed in a barge drawn by a single horse. By 1880, over 1 million tonnes of white salt and 100,000 tonnes of rock salt were being shipped down the Weaver annually.

Hunt's Locks stand on the site of one of the original 11 locks built by the Weaver Navigation Trust. In the late 1800s they were doubled up to allow two-way traffic and so speed up the movement of barges along the navigation.

5 Cross the locks via the footbridges, then go left for a few yards on the far side before bearing right along a surfaced footpath that leads to a swing footbridge spanning the old course of the River Weaver. This gives boat access to a dry dock situated beneath one of the viaduct arches along the river to the left. Turn left on the far side along a well-made footpath beside the river to a fork in

the path just in front of the viaduct and take the left-hand option, passing beneath the viaduct to reach Hunt's Locks Sluice and Dock Road Edwardian Pumping Station.

E. Edwardian Pumping Station

Built in 1913 to pump sewage from Northwich to the treatment works at Wallerscote, this lovely little building with its rare gas engines and pumps has now been fully restored to working order and can be seen in operation on weekends from Easter to the end of September, 2–5pm. Prior to its construction, sewage was discharged, untreated, directly into the river causing serious health and pollution problems.

Edwardian pumping station

6 Return to the viaduct and go left along a track leading to London Road. To discover the whole history of salt in Northwich turn left along the road for 200 yards to reach the Salt Museum. This occupies Weaver Hall; built as a workhouse in 1837 it is now completely devoted to the explanation and interpretation of the salt industry. To continue, cross London Road with care and walk alongside the viaduct to a bridge spanning the River Dane and bear right on the far side to join a broad, surfaced track now on the right-hand side of

the arches. Towards the end of a small park on the right, go left at a footpath sign, through a tunnel beneath the railway line, then bear right through Northwich Cemetery and past the impressive parish church of St Helen to reach the A559 dual carriageway.

7 Turn right beside the dual carriageway, cross Station Road, then cross towards the Mill House Inn before turning right along the opposite side of the A559. Proceed for about ½ mile, cross Denton Drive then, after a further 50 yards, go left alongside a tyre and exhaust fitters to join a rough track leading down to a bridge spanning Wincham Brook. Bear right on the far side, then swing sharp left over another bridge and walk alongside a drainage channel to reach a flight of steps leading up to a stile on the right after 100 yards. Pass between rustic posts and proceed ahead along the right-hand side of a field, climb a stile onto a grassy track alongside factory units and, where this enters a field, bear slightly left alongside a fence to reach the towpath of the Trent and Mersey Canal (there is a footbridge beside the canal). Turn left alongside the canal to reach the Lion Salt Works in Marston.

F. Lion Salt Works

This is the sole surviving example of an establishment that produced white salt by the original pre-Roman open-pan method. Wild brine, a concentrated salt solution several times saltier than sea water, is pumped up from underground streams into large iron salt pans. These are heated up, evaporating the water and allowing salt crystals to form which are then shovelled into tubs to form 14lb blocks, which are dried, cut and sold.

8 To visit the museum or the Salt Barge Inn, first pass beneath Bridge No 193 then go left along the road. Otherwise continue along the towpath

The Lion Salt Works

where the effects of natural-brine pumping can be seen in the surrounding landscape. Flooded 'flashes' and tilted or crumbling buildings are a result of subsidence from this old extraction method. The tow path runs past Marbury Country Park and Anderton Marina before crossing a bridge spanning the lock system leading to the Anderton Boat Lift.

G. Anderton Boat Lift
This marvellous piece of Victorian ingenuity and engineering was constructed in 1875 to link the Trent and Mersey Canal with the River Weaver and replace a labour-intensive and time-consuming chute system. It originally operated on a hydraulic system with two counter-balanced water-tight tanks raising and lowering boats between the two waterways, but was electrified in 1908 and the system modified so that the tanks could be operated independently. This system worked well until 1983 when severe corrosion of the main support legs forced British Waterways to shut the lift down. A renovation programme is now underway and it is hoped that the lift will be returned to full working order.

9 Continue along the towpath, passing beneath the A533 to reach a footbridge spanning the canal, at which point you leave this lovely waterway by going left down a surfaced walkway to reach the road. Cross to the swing bridge over the River Weaver and proceed along Winnington Lane, passing the massive soda crystal plant on the left before crossing Winnington Bridge.

H. The End of the Civil War

In 1659 the last battle of the English Civil War took place here when the Royalists, lead by Sir George Booth, were defeated by a detachment of Cromwell's New Model Army, commanded by General Lambert.

10 Walk on past the ICI works, where brine from the salt deposits is used to manufacture alkali products for the glass, soap, paper, textile, drug and dye-making industries, and follow the road back to Town Bridge in Northwich.

Parking:	Free parking near Town Bridge
Public Transport:	Buses from Altrincham, Chester, Crewe and Warrington, Tel: 01606 815050; trains Chester – Manchester, Tel: 08459 484950
Refreshments:	Pubs, cafés etc in Northwich; inn at Marston
Tourist Information:	1 The Arcade, Northwich CW9 5AS, Tel: 01606 353534
Salt Museum:	Open Tues – Fri 10–5pm, Sat and Sun 2–5pm, Tel: 01606 41331
Lion Salt Works:	Open 1.30–4.30pm daily, Tel: 01606 41823

WALK 15

Peckforton Castle

*Spurstow – Beeston Moss – Peckforton Castle –
Stanner Nab – Higher Burwardsley – Peckforton*

Distance:	6 miles (9.7km)
Start and Finish:	Spurstow
Maps:	OS Explorer 257 (Crewe and Nantwich)

Cheshire has more than its fair share of historic buildings but none quite like the splendid folly castle at Peckforton. This 19th-century castle was built to a historically accurate medieval design, and re-enactments add even more realism to this fabulous masquerade. It was the vision of John Tollemache, Member of Parliament for Cheshire and the largest landowner in the county in the 1870s. After visiting the castle, the lovely estate villages of Higher Burwardsley and Peckforton, with their individually designed workers cottages and houses, are visited.

Cyclists pedal through Spurstow, the start of the walk

The Peckforton hills have been important to man for over 3500 years with Bronze Age people first extracting their copper-rich rocks and soils for smelting. The villages of Burwardsley and Peckforton are both estate villages with attractive workers' dwellings.

1 From the cross-roads on the A49 in Spurstow, take the road towards Peckforton for 200 yards then turn right along a narrow lane with a footpath sign pointing to Beeston. Pass the Methodist chapel on the left and continue towards Haycroft Farm with the castellated towers of Peckforton Castle soon coming into view directly ahead. Keep left of the farm buildings, climb a stile beside a gate and walk round the left edge of two large fields; the silhouette of Peckforton Castle juts above the trees on its wooded hilltop, and the medieval Beeston Castle is clearly visible on top of its own craggy summit.

A. The Finest View in Cheshire?

Many regard this as the finest view in Cheshire and one of the most romantic in England, especially when the sun sinks in the western sky and a pink glow adds a colourful backdrop to this unique scene.

2 At the far end of the second field, climb a stile and negotiate the tiny River Gowy, which usually has a few well-placed stones to assist dry-shod crossing, then walk along an enclosed footpath between trees to reach Moss Cottage. Just beyond the cottage, bear left off the drive onto another enclosed footpath then, at a junction of paths by a multi-fingered signpost, go left over a stile beside a gate and along the left edge of two fields. Towards the far end of the second field, bear slightly right to a stile over a fence set alongside trees at Beeston Moss, then walk across a broad pasture, heading to the left of Peckforton Castle perched on the hill directly ahead. Cross a narrow footbridge over a brook, followed by a rough track and stiles. Now bear right and walk alongside Willis's Wood to a fence corner at the end of the wood, then bear diagonally left across a large, open meadow to a stile in the far left corner that leads onto the road just left of the Lodge. Go right to the Lodge, through the archway and onto the drive leading to Peckforton Castle.

The Lodge, Peckforton Castle

B. Peckforton Castle Lodge

The Lodge is a splendid building in its own right with arched windows, a single round tower crowned with a conical roof, arrow slits and a fine archway that presents the visitor with a taste of what is to come.

123

Peckforton Castle framed in a stone doorway

3 Walk along the drive, through a gateway, past a raised barrier and on through mature woodland to eventually reach the castle.

C. Peckforton Castle

Unlike its medieval neighbour, Beeston (just half a mile to the north), Peckforton is a mock castle, having been built in the mid 1800s. However, it is a real castle in the sense that it has been constructed in a true medieval style on an advantageous hilltop position. It was built by John Tollemache, Member of Parliament for Cheshire, between 1844 and 1851 to the designs of Anthony Salvin. It is of such architectural accuracy (with its towers and turrets, castellated ramparts, solid walls pierced with arrow slits and tortuous spiral staircases) that it's difficult to believe that it does not stem from the age of chivalry.

In fact, Salvin created such a historically perfect structure, that is so stark and inhuman, that for much of its life it has been unoccupied! On certain weekends through the summer months, medieval re-enactments add yet another touch of realism to this Victorian masquerade.

4 After visiting, return along the drive to the raised barrier, turn sharp right onto a footpath that rises steadily beneath trees that cloak the Peckforton hills and continue past Stanner Nab where the footpath levels out for a short distance before descending down the western slopes.

5 At a junction with a track, turn left for 50 yards then go right and descend steep steps to a junction with another track, which is followed to the left. Just beyond a gate the track joins a surfaced lane past attractive cottages and houses in Higher Burwardsley before reaching a crossroads just beyond the Pheasant Inn.

D. Burwardsley

Burwardsley is a lovely little village with magnificent views across the flood plains of the River Dee and into Wales. Many of the farms and houses in the village are owned by the Bolesworth Estate Company which is administered by the Barbour family, originally cotton magnates from Manchester. The Pheasant Inn was built during the 17th century and was previously known as the Cardon Arms. It is an excellent hostelry with a beer garden that takes full advantage of the splendid views.

6 Turn left, then left again at another crossroads. Keep right at a Y-fork and continue to eventually join a rough track that traverses a section of the Peckforton hills known as Waste Hill.

E. Bronze-Age Settlement

These uplands contain fairly high levels of copper ore that may have been mined as long ago as the Bronze

The view west into Wales from Higher Burwardsley

Age, around 1500 BC. The last attempt to extract copper took place in the 19th century, but cheap foreign imports put an end to any serious mining adventures here. The Romans quarried sandstone here in order to construct their roads and buildings; much of the stone in Beeston Castle was extracted from this site and, more recently, that in Peckforton Castle too.

7 Just beyond a bridge, climb a pair of stiles on the right then bear left, away from the wall on the right, and across the centre of a field with splendid views across the Cheshire Plain towards the misty blue hills of the Peak District. Descend past a pair of isolated trees to a fence corner where the path continues ahead (alongside the fence) to a stile beside a gate. Then bear slightly right, round the top of a small, sloping field to another stile leading into a long, narrow meadow. At the far end, climb a stile through a hedge, walk through an overgrown plantation, then bear left along a stony track, past a lovely thatched cottage and onto the road in Peckforton.

F. The Tollemache Estate

Many of the large estates in England either expanded or modified their holdings in the early 1800s and none more so than here at Peckforton. In 1846 the Tollemache estate had 45 tenants with various sized holdings; by 1850 many had been removed and replaced by a smaller number of newer units. At the same time, a number of tenanted cottages were demolished while others were refurbished in the very distinctive Tollemache style: diamond-latticed windows; timber frames with warm pink-brick infills; tall, elegant chimneys; and many with a bonnet of thatch. By the 1870s, John Tollemache was the largest landowner in Cheshire with his Peckforton estate amounting to 25,380 acres – almost 6% of Cheshire! He supplied each of his labourers with a cottage and three acres to supplement their living and was praised by Joseph Chamberlain, Mayor of Birmingham during the late nineteenth century, and Prime Minister William Gladstone as being a model landlord.

8 Turn right along the road for a short distance then go left along the road leading to Bunbury. This is a quiet, hedge-lined lane that runs past the solid buildings at Manor Farm, then on between fields before returning to Spurstow.

Parking:	Discreet roadside parking in Spurstow
Public Transport:	Huxley Travel Services C37 and C83 Chester – Barrow – Kelsall – Bunbury (no Sunday service), Tel: 01244 602666
Refreshments:	Pubs at Spurstow and Higher Burwardsley; café at Peckforton Castle
Tourist Information:	Town Hall, Northgate Street, Chester CH1 2HJ, Tel: 01244 402111; Chester Visitor Centre, Vicars Lane, Chester CH1 1QX, Tel: 01244 351609
Peckforton Castle:	Open daily from Easter until mid-Sept 10–6pm, Tel: 01829 260930

WALK 16

Stretton Watermill

*Farndon – Marsh Lane – Barton – Stretton Mill –
Stretton – Wetreins Green – Crewe Hill – River Dee*

Distance:	8¾ miles (14km)
Start and Finish:	Church Lane car park, Farndon
Maps:	OS Explorer 257 (Crewe and Nantwich)

On the western extremities of the county, the River Dee forms the boundary between England and Wales. This fairly long but gentle walk explores the rich, flat lands and pretty villages on the English side of the border and allows you to enjoy a visit to a splendid working watermill before returning along the Dee itself.

Farndon is an attractive village on the banks of the River Dee and an important bridging point between England and Wales, while Farndon church, which had to be rebuilt following the Civil War, contains some lovely stained-glass windows. Stretton Mill is one of the county's best-kept secrets, being a working watermill operated by two separate water wheels.

1 Turn left out of the car park, passing the lovely parish church of St Chad on the right.

A. St Chad

It is quite fitting that this lovely church should be dedicated to St Chad, who died in 672 BC, as he was the first Bishop of Mercia, the Anglo-Saxon kingdom covering most of central England, including Cheshire. There may well have been buildings on this sandstone ridge as far back as Celtic times, but the outline of the present building dates from the 1300s. During the Civil War the church was used as barracks for some 2000 Roundheads intent upon invading the Royalist stronghold of Wales. During the ensuing battles the church caught fire and was severely damaged and, apart from the tower, had to be completely rebuilt.

2 At a junction with Barton Road, cross straight over onto a lane between cottages (footpath sign to Churton) and follow this onto a narrow footpath leading into fields on the outskirts of Farndon. Walk along the left side of a field and cross the next short field, but instead of passing through the gate turn right alongside the field hedge, continuing ahead at the hedge corner to a stile leading onto the B5130.

3 Turn left along the road for 120 yards, then go right along the drive to Sibbersfield Lane Farm (signposted to Churton and

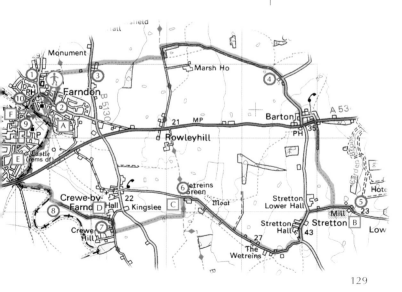

Coddington), keeping left of all the farm buildings to join a concrete track between fields. At the end of the track, pass through a gate then bear diagonally left across a pasture to a plank footbridge and stile in the far left corner, leading into another pasture and walk down the left side of this to a kissing gate. This leads onto a broad, grassy track known as Marsh Lane, which is followed to the left for 150 yards before turning right along a similar green track (signposted to Coddington). Follow the track to its end where it joins a country lane.

4 Turn right, along the lane and into the pretty little hamlet of Barton with its attractive houses and thatched cottages. Turn left in the village, following the road round to the right to a junction with the busy A534. Cross with care onto a track beside a house leading into a field and walk down the right-hand side of this and, after two-thirds of the way along the hedge, go over a stile. Once over, turn left along the adjacent field to another stile 30 yards from the field end, then go right on the opposite side, continuing ahead at a hedge

The lovingly restored Stretton Watermill

corner to reach an awkward stile on the far side of the field. This leads onto the newly developed Carden Park Golf Course, one of the largest golf courses in England with two 18-hole and one 9-hole course. Bear left, past newly planted trees, then veer right across two fairways (check on the state of any play first) to a hedge on the opposite side and follow this to the left to a hedge corner and an old stile. Bear right alongside another hedge, with a large ornamental lake over to the left, to a junction with a lane and go left along this for 300 yards to reach Stretton Watermill.

B. Stretton Watermill

This beautifully restored mill provides an evocative glimpse of a way of life that has now all but disappeared. Records show that a mill existed on this site as early as the 14th century, but the present structure dates from the 1600s with modifications in the 1700s and 1800s. The mill finally ceased its commercial operations in 1959 and started to fall into decay until salvaged and repaired by the Cheshire County Council. The current miller is Dave Maddocks, a local retired bobby who gives fascinating tours and talks on the structure of the mill and the milling processes, including working demonstrations of the mill's two water wheels and associated machinery.

5 After visiting the mill, retrace your steps along the lane and continue to a junction with another lane and go left through the attractive hamlet of Stretton, passing its splendid halls and well-tended gardens. At the far end of the hamlet and by the gated drive leading to Stretton Hall, turn right into the quiet hedge-lined Wetreins Lane and follow this for a little over 1 mile to Wetreins Green Farm.

6 Turn left just beyond the farm onto a byway signposted to Castletown and walk along this for 300 yards to a stile and footpath sign on the right.

Unusual stock for this hemisphere, ostriches

C. Green Lanes

This is an old green lane that has been in use for centuries. In times past it would have resounded to the rattle of carts drawn by oxen, the bellowing of cattle on their way to market and the clanking of pots and pans hanging from the carriages and caravans of travellers.

7 Climb the stile then walk across three fields to a road, bearing diagonally right to a stile on the opposite side before crossing two more fields to reach a quiet lane opposite a white-painted cottage. Go right along the lane for 200 yards, then turn left onto a broad track signposted to Farndon.

D. Ostriches!

As you pass beside the fields of Crewe Hall Farm on the right, you may notice rather unusual stock for the northern hemisphere – ostriches!

8 At the end of the track, walk along the right edge of a field to reach the tree-lined banks of the River Dee. Turn right alongside the Dee (fine views across Wales to the Clwydian hills) and follow the riverside footpath all the way back to Farndon.

E. Border Castles

The ruins of Holt Castle can be seen on the opposite

bank shortly after passing beneath the A534. This was an important Royalist stronghold during the Civil War but, unfortunately, little remains of the structure today.

9 Close to Farndon the path is squeezed between the river and ancient red sandstone cliffs on a series of wooden duckboards before opening out near the splendid medieval bridge spanning the Dee between England and Wales.

F. Geological Time

The sandstone cliffs were deposited 245 million years ago in the Triassic period when sand, silt and grit (eroded from the Welsh and Pennine uplands) were washed into a large inland sea covering this part of the country. Much of the stone has been quarried in the past and is present in many of the local buildings, especially Farndon Bridge. Farndon has always been an important crossing point on the Dee and one that has been fought over from Roman times through to the Civil War. The present bridge was built in the 1300s and, depending on which side of the river you reside, is either known as Farndon Bridge or Holt Bridge.

10 Turn right at the bridge and right again just beyond the public toilets to return to the car park.

Parking:	See Start and Finish
Public Transport:	Service 56 Chester – Wrexham (not Sundays)
Refreshments:	Pubs in Farndon; inn at Barton (evenings and Sunday lunch only); café in Holt
Tourist Information:	Town Hall, Northgate Street, Chester CH1 2HJ, Tel: 01244 402111; Chester Visitors Centre, Vicars Lane, Chester CH1 1QX, Tel: 01244 351609
Stretton Mill:	May – August, 1–5pm daily (closed Mon except BH Mondays); April – Sept weekends only, Tel: Cheshire Museums Service 01606 41331

WALK 17

Tatton Park

*Knutsford – Tatton Mere – Melchett Mere –
Tatton Hall – Old Hall – Dog Wood – Knutsford*

Distance:	6 miles (9.7km)
Start and Finish:	Tourist Information Centre, Knutsford
Map:	OS Explorer 268 (Wilmslow, Macclesfield and Congleton)

Tatton Park, with its charming meres, landscaped parkland, enchanting gardens and splendid mansion is the perfect setting for a relaxing stroll. This easy walk from the lovely town of Knutsford links up areas of historic and natural interest, exploring some of the quieter areas of the park; any dog that likes water will be in its element!

Knutsford is a very pleasant town that will more than satisfy those in need of retail therapy, while Tatton Park is a magnificent mix of woodland, lakes, open grassland and formal gardens. The mansion at Tatton is

Tatton Mere

of a neo-classical design, built around 1800; numerous special events take place here throughout the year.

1 From the TI Office go left and cross Toft Road via the pedestrian lights; continue left on the far side with the Session House opposite.

A. The Session House

This is a marvellously proportioned building of the early Greek revival style, built in the early 1800s. The town gaol once stood behind the Session House and housed up to 700 prisoners, in what one can only imagine as being less than humane conditions; the Governor lived a more opulent lifestyle in the Georgian building that now serves as the Council Offices and Tourist Information Centre.

2 Turn right down Church Hill, passing the parish church of John the Baptist, which was built in 1744 following a campaign by the good Christian folk of the town to separate them from the Parish of Rostherne.

At the bottom, go left along King Street with its fine range of shops, pubs and cafés and past the Gaskell Memorial Tower and Heritage Centre.

3 Just beyond Drury Lane, bear right on a good footpath leading into Tatton Park and to a junction with Knutsford Drive, the main access into the park from the south. Lewis Wyatt, the architect responsible for much of the design of the main house, designed the fine Doric arch here. Once through the arch, pass through an iron pedestrian gate, bear right over a drive leading to a parking area and along a grassy footpath; Tatton Mere soon comes into view. Head on towards the mere and join a good footpath along its western shore.

B. Tatton Park

Tatton Park extends over some 2000 acres, 1000 of which are open to the public. Despite there being no rights of way in the park, numerous footpaths, tracks and drives allow the visitor to wander at will during opening times, except where gates or signs specifically prohibit entry. Tatton Mere is the largest sheet of water in the park, and besides being home to a variety of birds and waterfowl, it is also used by the Tatton Outdoor and Sailing Centre; their craft add bright splashes of colour to the landscape. Mallard, coot, moorhen, tufted ducks, swans, grebes, various gulls and even cormorants can be seen here, and during the autumn and winter months great flocks of Canada geese fly in to feed.

4 On approaching the far end of the mere, bear left across the parkland to join Knutsford Drive and go right along this, with one of the finest views in Tatton opening up to the left.

C. Tatton Hall

Across the tranquil Melchett Mere and over the beautifully landscaped parkland you can see Tatton's splendid mansion, set in a framework of mature trees. The building that can be seen here today is the last in a series of dwellings that have served the masters of Tatton. It has been rebuilt, altered and extended many times over the years, but its fundamental character is neo-classical, a style popular in the early 1800s.

5 Shortly after passing the end of Melchett Mere, bear left off the drive along the edge of an enclosed stand of trees and round the northern edge of the mere. Eventually the grassy path swings rightwards towards the house but, at a junction with a broad track, go left through a gateway in a wire fence. The path swings gently left to reach the garden boundary, marked by a ha-ha (ditch) and wire fence with the Choragic Monument of Lysicrates on the far side.

Tatton Hall

D. Choragic Monument

The folly was commissioned in 1820 by Wilbraham Egerton after being inspired by the monument to the story-teller Lysicrates in ancient Athens. It was originally surrounded by steps and a balustrade; these were removed in 1965 after brine extraction caused subsidence.

6 Bear right off the main track and follow a grassy footpath round the southern perimeter of the garden. Pass through a gateway in a wire fence and proceed to an awkward stile through the deer fence. Walk ahead on an obvious path through woodland, across grassy pasture, passing to the left of a wall jutting out into the field and heading for a pair of gates left of a children's playground. Go through either gate, walk along the edge of the main car park and then turn right along the path signposted to the restaurant and mansion. This leads into the stableyard where you can obtain refreshment, and enter the gardens and visit the house.

The Stableyard, Tatton

E. Tatton's Gardens

Tatton's 60 acres of gardens are regarded as some of the finest in the country with Italian, Japanese and rose gardens; statues, lawns, pools, fountains and flower-filled borders; an arboretum, orangery and fernery. At the time of writing, Tatton's walled gardens, which once provided flowers, fruit and vegetables for the house, are being restored.

7 After visiting, repasting or simply resting, walk round to the front of the mansion to a Y-fork in the road; go right along the drive signposted to Old Hall. The terminal buildings and cargo storage areas at Manchester Airport can be seen to the left. After 300 yards, bear diagonally left off the drive and head across open parkland towards a large stand of trees that hides the Old Hall, your next destination.

F. Old Hall

This was originally the medieval manor house, built at the end of the Middle Ages for the lords of Tatton, and was the most important building in the area for several hundred years. Despite the fairly modern-looking exterior, the interior (with its atmospheric and impressive original great hall) soon whisks you back in time to the medieval period. Other rooms in the house have been restored to reflect the different periods in the hall's history. The 17th-century barn, moved here in 1978, is also a splendid building.

8 After visiting, return to the access drive and go left. At a T-junction with another drive in front of Tatton Mere, go left for 100 yards then right, past a barrier and along a track giving sailing craft access to the lake. Continue along a grassy footpath on the eastern shore of the mere with fabulous views over the park.

G. Wildlife Habitats

Tatton's parkland has remained relatively undisturbed, and what we see today is mainly the work of Humphrey Repton, an architect commissioned to landscape the park at the same time that Samuel Wyatt started work on the mansion. The result is numerous wildlife habitats, including wetland, woodland and open parkland. Besides the sheep and cattle that graze here, the most visible animals are the fallow and red deer. The genetic line of the 800 animals in the park runs back to the original herd, established here by Sir Richard Massey in the 13th century.

9 The lakeside footpath eventually bears slightly left, through Dog Wood, to reach a tall gate through the deer fence. Once through, proceed along a broad track that leads out of the park, then crosses the railway line via a humpback bridge. Walk along Mallard Close, turn right along Teal Avenue then go right again along the main road. At the pedestrian lights, turn right down Middle Walk, pass beneath the railway line then walk ahead through a park and past the Moor Pool. Cross Moorside on the far side of the park, walk up Malt Street back into King Street and retrace your steps back to the start.

Parking:	Plentiful in Knutsford
Public Transport:	Buses from Altrincham, Chester, Macclesfield, Northwich, Warrington, Tel: 01625 534850; trains from Chester, Altrincham, Stockport, Tel: 08459 48 49 50
Tourist Information:	Council Offices, Toft Road, Knutsford WA16 6TA, Tel: 01565 632611
Tatton Park:	National Trust, park open Tues – Sun 11–5pm in winter. House closed, except for special Christmas events, Tel: 01625 534435

WALK 18
Walton Hall

*Higher Walton – Bridgewater Canal –
Moore – Row's Wood – Hatton – Walton Hall*

Distance:	5½ miles (9km)
Start and Finish:	Car park at Walton Hall (grid ref: SJ600852)
Map:	OS Explorer 276 Bolton (Wigan and Warrington)

This gentle walk in the fertile countryside to the south of Warrington provides the opportunity to enjoy two features from the area's industrial past. These are the Bridgewater Canal (the granddaddy of our canal network), constructed to transport coal, and Walton Hall, built from the profits of beer!

Walton Hall was built in the Elizabethan style for Edward Greenall, a member of the famous Greenall

The Walton Arms

Whitley brewing business, and now forms part of a very popular country park and garden. The Bridgewater Canal, named after the Duke of Bridgewater, was the first of its type to be built in England. Moore, Hatton and Higher Walton are all attractive villages that offer refreshment in their cosy inns.

1 From the car park, bear right along the access road towards the village of Higher Walton, with the church of St John the Evangelist over to the right; it was once described as 'a cathedral in miniature'.

A. St John the Evangelist
This was built in 1885 at the expense of Sir Gilbert Greenall of Walton Hall, a devout Anglican. It is a magnificent building, decorated in a Gothic style, with an impressive crossing tower supporting a recessed spire that is 130ft tall and dominates the landscape hereabouts.

2 Continue past attractive cottages, draped with the grape-like blooms of Wisteria in the spring, towards the village centre.

B. Higher Walton
Though not mentioned in the Domesday Book, Higher Walton is recorded in 1190 as 'Waletona' and held by Herbert de Walton from a Lord Daresbury. It remained a relatively small agricultural hamlet until the 1800s when several houses, along with the church, Walton school and village hall, were constructed for the estate workers of

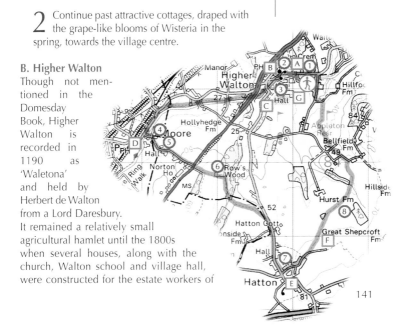

Attractive narrow boats line the Bridgewater Canal

Walton Hall. The Walton Arms, known as the Bay Horse Inn prior to 1880, was a famous refreshment stop for passengers on a horse-drawn packet boat that used to travel along the Bridgewater Canal at weekends and public holidays.

3 Just before the road junction in the village, go left through a gap in railings onto the towpath of the canal and go right along this, passing numerous brightly coloured narrow and pleasure boats, towards Moore.

C. Bridgewater Canal

The Bridgewater Canal was built in 1762 and was the first canal to be built entirely independent of any river system. It was designed to link the Duke of Bridgewater's collieries at Worsley with the Mersey at Runcorn, so avoiding the Mersey and Irwell Navigation and allowing the Duke's coal to be sent direct to Liverpool and Manchester at a greatly reduced cost. It soon became an extremely busy waterway, not only for coal but for heavy freight and agricultural produce. Today it is one of the most popular recreational waterways in the country, with all kinds of pleasure craft and narrow boats cruising its tranquil waters.

4 Turn right 30 yards after passing beneath Moore Bridge (name on parapet on far side) and double back to cross the bridge; to explore Moore or visit the popular Red Lion Inn, bear left (instead of right) at the road and go along the road into the village.

D. Moore

Moore is an attractive village with a number of fine houses and cottages situated on low-lying land in the Mersey Valley. Most of the surrounding land has been drained and farmed for centuries, but because of its relative ease of access, the area has seen the building of some of Cheshire's most important routeways. The Manchester Ship Canal now forms the northern boundary to the village, two important railway lines cut through its centre, while to the south and east lie the Bridgewater Canal, the A558 Runcorn road and the main A56 road between Chester and Warrington. Despite all this, the central part of the village is now a conservation area; Village Farm, the oldest building here, dates from the 1600s.

The footpath runs alongside Row's Wood near Moore

5 Once over Moore Bridge, walk along Hobb Lane, passing the

reputedly haunted buildings of Moore Hall over to the right, to a junction with the A56 Chester Road. Cross with care onto a broad, sandy track running through the middle of fields to reach a triple-fingered footpath sign at the corner of Outer Wood and bear diagonally left through the middle of fields, heading towards Row's Wood, with fine views over Warrington and the West Pennine Moors beyond.

6 Pass through a kissing gate on the far side of the fields, then walk round the right edge of Row's Wood, a private woodland that is carpeted with the most wonderful display of bluebells in April and May (no picking!) and alive with birdsong throughout the year. Almost at the far end of the wood, go left through a kissing gate in a rustic fence and follow the obvious track through the trees, which crosses a small stream before exiting into a meadow on the far side. Walk along its right edge, pass through a kissing gate in the far hedge and proceed through the next meadow, keeping an eye on the sky for the local buzzards that frequently circle above these fields. Keep left through a third, narrow meadow to reach Warrington Road and turn right along this into Hatton.

E. Hatton

This little settlement has been in existence since at least 1230 when it was first mentioned as being given by Geoffrey, son of Adam of Dutton, to William, son of Hothy of Hatton. Until the 1900s, the hamlet consisted of mainly isolated farms and farm labourers' cottages, but in recent years, residential housing has been built along Goose Lane and Warrington Road. It is now something of a dormitory village, with the Warrington New Town development reaching ever closer as it sprawls southwards through Cheshire's green and pleasant land. Between the First and Second World Wars, gangs of Irish potato-pickers would arrive in the village and work with the local women, picking and bagging potatoes. They were accommodated in out-buildings and lean-tos known as paddy-shants, a feature of many of the area's farms at the time.

7 Turn left by the Hatton Arms into Goose Lane, which eventually becomes a rough track. Where this swings round to the right towards Stretton, continue ahead, passing to the left of a gate and joining a footpath signposted to Stockton Heath.

F. Delamere Way
This is part of the Delamere Way, an obvious and clearly waymarked long-distance trail that starts near Frodsham before forming a loop which takes in the Overton hills, sections of the Delamere Forest and Weaver Valley.

8 These quiet field paths then lead towards Stockton Heath on the outskirts of Warrington. The path eventually joins a rough track through a belt of trees where pheasants forage and bluebells thrive, to reach a junction with a made-up track just before a house. Go left along this for 150 yards to a left-hand bend in the track. Here bear right onto a footpath through a young copse of trees and across heathland with orange-tip, common blue, gatekeeper and peacock butterflies fluttering through the summer air. Cross a lane to join the well-marked continuation footpath through a golf course. On the far side, go right along a red gravel track, cross a stream then bear left across grass to a kissing gate leading onto a lane. Turn left along this, go right at the T-junction with Hough's Lane, passing the grounds of Walton Hall on the left, and at the next T-junction turn left and follow it back to the car park or the entrance of Walton Hall Park and Gardens.

G. Walton Hall

Walton Hall was built in the Elizabethan style for Edward Greenall in the 1830s, extended by his son, Sir Gilbert Greenall, in the 1870s and again by his grandson, Lord Daresbury, at the end of the 19th century. The lands which made up the 7000 acre Walton Estate were acquired by the Greenall family in 1814, and by the time Lord Daresbury died in 1938 Walton had become a model agricultural village. Lady Daresbury was an enthusiastic gardener who, with the aid of 26 grounds-men and a pony-drawn lawn mower, converted the grounds around the hall into a miniature Kew, famed for its spectacular azaleas and rhododendrons, rare trees, formal borders, verdant lawns and greenhouses filled with exotic plants.

The park and gardens today, despite many changes, still retain much of their former splendour with colourful blooms, trees and shrubs from all over the world, well-tended lawns and ornamental ponds. Add to this picnic areas, a children's playground, crazy golf, pitch 'n' put, a bowling green, café, heritage centre and even a well-loved children's zoo, and it soon becomes clear why Walton is a popular venue for a family day out.

Parking:	See Start and Finish
Public Transport:	Buses from Warrington and Runcorn to Higher Walton, Tel: 01925 444250
Refreshments:	Pubs in Higher Walton, Hatton and Moore; café at Walton Hall
Tourist Information:	Market Hall, Academy Way, Warrington WA1 2EN, Tel: 01925 632571

Walton Hall Park and Gardens:

Open every day of the year, 8am to dusk; attractions normally open at 10.30am, Tel: 01925 601617

WALK 19

*Warrington and
the Manchester Ship Canal*

*Warrington – River Mersey – Paddington Meadows –
Thelwall Eye – Manchester Ship Canal – Victoria Park*

Distance:	7½ miles (12km)
Start and Finish:	Orchard Square, Warrington
Map:	OS Explorer 276 (Bolton, Wigan and Warrington)

This is an interesting walk that mixes both urban and rural landscapes in and around Warrington, including stretches along the River Mersey and a fine section of the Manchester Ship Canal; there is a chance to witness the movement of ocean-going ships through the impressive Latchford Locks.

Warrington's history goes back some 10,000 years when our early ancestors developed a crossing point

*Golden Gates,
Sankey Street*

147

over the River Mersey here. The town has a number of very interesting buildings, including the Old Barley Mow Inn, which dates from 1561. The Manchester Ship Canal, opened in 1894 by Queen Victoria, is 36 miles long, while Thelwall Eye, a man-made lake, is a good place to watch wildfowl.

A. Warrington

Warrington has been a settlement since about 8000 BC, when early man established a crossing point over the River Mersey which remained the only major crossing of the river until the middle of the 13th century. During Roman times, the most complex and extensive Roman site in the county outside Chester was at Wilderspool, just south of the Warrington and known as Veratinum. This was not a military site, although a fort on the north bank of the Mersey at Warrington seems likely. It was instead a large industrial and trading centre which had excellent road links to Chester, Wigan, Northwich, Middlewich, Whitchurch and Manchester and, being at the head of navigation on the river at that time, became a trans-shipment point for the import and export of goods. Since these early times, Warrington has been noted for its diversity of industries, a quality that the town still retains.

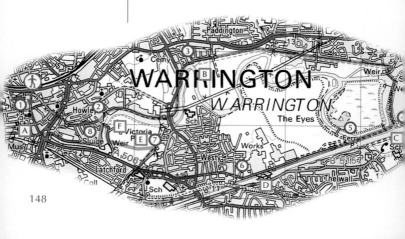

Today, the principal streets in the town are predominantly Georgian in style, with some fine examples of Georgian town houses along Sankey Street and in the Old Market Square. Also on Sankey Street is the town hall, formerly known as Bank Hall, a splendid house built as the country seat of the Patten family in 1750, when the area was nothing but green fields with open views towards the River Mersey. The property was sold to the Warrington Corporation in 1873 and now houses the council chamber, mayor's parlour and various committee rooms. At the front of the town hall is a set of magnificent gilded, cast-iron gates known as the Golden Gates. They were made at Ironbridge in Shropshire and intended for erection outside Queen Victoria's Sandringham Estate, but instead were purchased for the town in 1895.

1 From Orchard Square, walk down Buttermarket Street to its junction with Academy Way, cross to the opposite side and turn right to reach Mersey Street. Go left for a few yards then cross via the pedestrian lights into Hall Street, alongside the Mersey Inn, follow this into Parr Street and almost at its end go right into Riverside Close. After 40 yards, turn left along an enclosed footpath that leads to the banks of the Mersey by an attractive footbridge spanning the river.

2 Keep left alongside the river with the massive spire of St Elphin's Church dominating the skyline ahead. At 281ft high it is the third tallest parish spire in England. The footpath soon becomes enclosed, swings away from the river then joins a road alongside industrial units. Keep right along this to eventually reach Howley Lane, a road that runs alongside the Mersey towards Warrington Rowing Club. Pass beneath Kingsway Bridge, continue alongside the river, keep right at the junction with a road (Paddington Bank), and at the end of this rejoin the riverside footpath which leads to Paddington Meadows Nature Reserve.

B. Paddington Meadows Nature Reserve

This green oasis of 74 acres is an important part of Warrington's history and the town's last remaining area of original riverside grassland, once typical of the whole river valley. The site is enclosed on three sides by a meander of the River Mersey, and to the north by the now disused Woolston New Cut. The site has been farmed in its current field pattern for at least 200 years and one of the most striking features are the huge hawthorn hedges, some of the oldest existing in Cheshire. Fertiliser is no longer used here so the varieties of wildflowers in the meadows should increase along with insects. A riverside path skirts the whole of the meadows and rejoins the main route a little further on.

An ocean-going vessel glides along the Manchester Ship Canal

3 Follow the footpath alongside the overgrown canal, eventually crossing two access drives, one to a refuse disposal site and one to industrial units. At a junction with a third drive, Weir Lane, turn right along it in the direction of the footpath sign to Latchford, but after a short distance go left over a broad wooden footbridge spanning the River Mersey. The two weirs on the river here were built to prevent the annual flooding of Warrington and to provide water for the region's canals. Climb the zigzag footpath on the far side to reach a broad track and go right along this with the waters of Thelwall Eye over the bank to the left. Part way along the track is

a bird hide, South Hide, which gives an opportunity to view the many waterfowl that use the Eye.

4 The track eventually descends and swings right, going between the River Mersey to the right and the Manchester Ship Canal to the left.

C. Manchester Ship Canal

On January 1 1894, the massive lock gates at Eastham on the River Mersey swung open and the Manchester Ship Canal (or the Big Ditch, as it was affectionately known) was open for business, allowing ships to sail the 36 miles into the heart of Manchester. Built between 1887 and 1894 at a cost of £15 million, a staggering sum at the time, the canal soon justified its construction with a rapid growth in trade which elevated Manchester to one of the major ports of the world and the third busiest in the UK by tonnage shipped along the waterway. The project involved the excavation of 77 million tonnes of rock and earth, the construction of five sets of massive locks, seven swing road bridges, the famous swing aqueduct at Barton, five high-level railway viaducts, the laying of miles of temporary railway track to service the excavation and the employment of 16,000 navvies, not all of whom were able to clock off at the end! At its completion, contemporary accounts described it as 'One of the greatest pieces of engineering known', in fact it was arguably the greatest engineering project of the Victorian era.

5 After a short distance you pass a little green hut belonging to Thelwall Ferry, a service which still operates today, before joining a surfaced lane alongside the canal that leads to the impressive Latchford Locks.

D. Latchford Locks

The locks on the Manchester Ship Canal are designed to take vessels up to 600ft long, 65ft wide and with a draught of 26ft. The multiple locks here allow vessels to pass along the canal in both directions at the same time.

Latchford Locks

In the late 18th century, roads in this area were little better than muddy tracks and the railways were exorbitantly expensive, factors which were stifling the industrial development of south and east Lancashire, a county to which Warrington once belonged. With the opening of the canal, trade in the area boomed and ships queued to pass through the locks here at Latchford.

6 At the far end of the locks bear right, away from the canal and past terraced houses in Thelwall Lane. Cross the A50 Kingsway and continue along Thelwall Lane until an iron gate on the right gives access to Victoria Park. Bear left through the park, passing old brick pavilions, to reach the main drive and turn right along it.

E. Victoria Park

This is Warrington's premier site for sport and houses the town's Multi-Sports Arena. Originally part of a private estate known as Old Warps, the park was purchased by the Warrington Corporation in 1897 and renamed Victoria Park to mark the Queen's jubilee year.

7 Alongside the toilet block, turn left to reach a broad track above the Mersey. Follow this rightwards to a footbridge over the river, with the original Old Warps Country House to the right.

F. Suspension Bridge

The bridge was built in 1912 and should have been a 60ft-wide road bridge, designed to relieve traffic at Bridge Foot in the town; however, lack of funds meant a slight scaling down of the original project, leaving us with this rather charming suspension bridge.

The suspension bridge linking town with Victoria Park

8 Once over, retrace your steps back into town or follow the riverside footpath (part of the Mersey Way) which leads to the A49, Mersey Street, south of the town.

Parking:	Plentiful in Warrington
Public Transport:	Trains and buses from Chester, Liverpool, Manchester, Runcorn and Northwich, Tel: 01925 632571
Refreshments:	All kinds in Warrington
Tourist Information:	The Market Hall, Academy Way, Warrington WA1 2EN, Tel: 01925 632571

WALK 20
Peover Hall

Lower Peover – Freegreen Farm –
Radbroke – Peover Hall – Meadowbank – Peover Eye

Distance:	5¾ miles (9.25km)
Start and Finish:	St Oswald's Church, Lower Peover
Maps:	OS Explorer 268 (Wilmslow, Macclesfield and Congleton)

It is hard to believe that this lovely part of Cheshire was described in the Domesday Book as being of little value and mostly waste. A very different story would be written today with scattered farms, pretty cottages, hidden hamlets and historic buildings nestling in the folds of what is now some of the county's most fertile land.

Lower Peover is a charming hamlet with a beautiful timber-framed church and a delightful inn that has been trading for centuries. Peover Hall, with its warm brickwork and Elizabethan lines, has evidence of occupation since medieval times. The sparkling stream, now called the Peover Eye, has links with early Britons and would have been an important navigation in ancient times.

Stained-glass windows in St Oswald's Church

A. St Oswald's Church

St Oswald's is one of the most beautiful churches in England and one of the few surviving timber-framed churches. The present building stands on the site of an early Saxon church (hence the dedication to St Oswald) which was founded in 1269. Most of the Cheshire 'magpie' construction is 14th century but the tower, added in 1582, is Tudor. This tower originally contained two bells but now there are six; all in regular use, their beautiful chimes carry for many miles across the sweet fields of Cheshire.

1 From the church, head north along Church Walk, crossing Peover Eye before ascending gently to a junction with a road. Go right, along this to another junction with Freegreen Lane. Turn right again, past lovely warm pink brick and white-washed cottages and on between lush fields.

2 When opposite the attractive black and white Freegreen Cottage, turn sharp left along a bri-dleway and through a small wood before passing alongside the solid buildings at Freegreen Farm. Continue along the surfaced drive, through a pedes-trian gate to the left of an iron farm gate and between buildings in the farmyard before joining Sandy Lane, a broad track running between fields. The track passes buildings at Sandylane Farm before a junction with the busy A50 which is crossed with care to a footpath on the opposite side. Turn right towards the Whipping Stocks Inn.

B. Coaching Inn

The inn was an important refreshment stop in the days of horse-drawn vehicles; as many as a dozen coaches a day halted

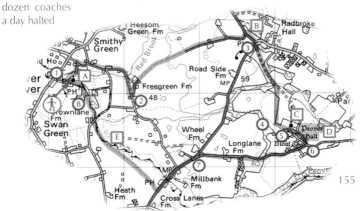

their journey here as they travelled to and from London, Liverpool, Scotland, Wales and the east coast. In the 16th century, the Court Leet was held here and there may also have been a medieval fair.

3 From the inn, go right for a few yards then left through white gates beside an old gate house and onto a broad track running through Peover Park. This is a lovely stretch of rich pasture land dotted with mature trees and once the hunting preserve of the Lords of the Manor of Over Peover. Shortly after crossing a stream between ponds, bear right at a Y-fork (waymarker) and continue for approximately 200 yards to a stile on the right leading into a rough pasture, with an enclosed conservation area directly ahead.

4 Turn left alongside the fence and continue to a stile on the left, leading into a field with a high brick wall surrounding part of the Peover Hall gardens directly ahead. Climb another stile on the right after 20 yards and follow the obvious stony footpath through mature woodland, past a variety of outbuildings, before reaching the path leading to the parish church of St Lawrence on the left.

C. Church of St Lawrence

The church, with its pleasing combination of brick and stonework, is believed to date from the 14th century. It was built as a private chapel of ease by the Mainwaring family, lords of the manor and benefactors of the church for over 800 years. As one would expect, this church, dominated by one family, contains many Mainwaring associations: two effigies of John and Margaret Mainwaring date back over 500 years. The alabaster effigy of Margaret is the oldest of its kind in Cheshire.

5 From the church, continue on towards the stable yard. Turn left through ornate iron gates at the end of the high wall then right along the rear of

the stables. These fine buildings date from the 1650s, the ground floor originally being divided by ornately carved Jacobean woodwork into 16 stalls overlooked by a fine plaster ceiling.

D. Peover Hall

To the left at this point is Peover Hall, a beautiful structure that forms the focal point of this lovely cluster of historic buildings. It was constructed in 1585 by Sir Ralph Mainwaring to replace an earlier half-timbered dwelling that stood on a moated site to the south. Despite its many mullioned windows and numerous gables, this lovely house is essentially Elizabethan in character with fine panelled walls, plasterwork ceilings and carved staircase. The surrounding gardens are well worth exploring.

6 At a junction with a broad track, turn right past more outbuildings then go left along the drive to a Y-fork and turn sharp right past St Anthony's Cottages. At the end of the lane, continue ahead along an enclosed and partly cobbled bridleway that eventually joins a surfaced lane leading to a junction with the Holmes Chapel Road.

7 Go left here, first along a footpath on the left-hand side of the road, then on the right and continue for ⅓ mile to the Drovers Arms, climbing a stile just beyond the inn into a field. **This next section follows a footpath diversion and is different from the current OS map.** Walk along the right edge of two fields then along the left edge of a third to a stile at the far end. Once over, head straight across the centre of the next small field. Climb a stile at the end of a rustic fence then walk along the top edge of the next two fields, bearing slightly right just before the end of the second field to a stile shrouded by holly trees. Join a narrow footpath, squeezed in between a fence and the Peover Eye, that leads to Foxcovert Lane. Cross the lane and continue along a pleasant section of

Peover Eye, the 'Sparkling Stream'

streamside footpath with St Oswald's Church tower visible across the meadows.

E. The Sparkling Stream

The name 'Peover Eye' derives from early British people, well before Roman times, who would have manoeuvred their coracles and primitive boats between the narrow banks as they traversed this part of Cheshire. Peover, pronounced as 'Peever', was formerly spelt 'Pever' or 'Pevr', which meant 'dart' but was also used to describe something sparkling or bright. The Anglo-Saxons added 'Ee', their word for stream, which has since been modified to 'Eye'. The Sparkling Stream – a perfect description!

8 Shortly after passing a wooden footbridge over the stream (sluice system to the right), follow the path through a gap in a cross fence, bearing left, away from the stream and across a broad meadow, heading back towards St Oswald's Church.

Parking:	Limited in village; rough lay-by on Freegreen Lane (grid ref. SJ745743)
Public Transport:	PMT Service E49 Sandbach – Northwich, Sat only; Baker's Coaches Service H50 Sandbach – Altrincham, Tues only, Tel: Cheshire Busline 01270 505350
Refreshments:	Inns at Lower Peover, Radbroke and Meadowbank
Tourist Information:	Council Offices, Toft Road, Knutsford WA16 6TA, Tel: 01565 632611
Peover Hall:	House, stables and gardens May – Sept, Mon only (but not BH Mondays), 2.30–4.30pm; stables and gardens only, Thurs 2-5pm, Tel: 01565 632358

APPENDIX:
Tourist Information Offices

Altringham	20 Stamford New Road, Altrincham WA14 1EJ Tel: 0161 912 5931, Fax: 0161 941 7089
Chester	Town Hall, Northgate Street, Chester CH1 2HJ Tel: 01244 318356
	Chester Visitor Centre, Vicars Lane, Chester CH11XQ Tel: 01244 351609
	Chester Railway Station, Station Road, Chester CH1 3W Tel: 01244 322220
Congleton	20 High Street, Congleton CW12 1BD Tel: 01260 271095
Knutsford	Council Offices, Toft Road, Knutsford WA16 6TA Tel: 01565 632611
Macclesfield	Council Offices, Town Hall, Macclesfield SK10 1DX Tel: 01625 504114
Nantwich	Church House, Church Walk, Nantwich, Cheshire CW5 5RG Tel: 01270 610983
Northwich	1 The Arcade, Northwich CW9 5AS Tel: 01606 353534
Poynton	83 Park Lane, Poynton SK12 1RD Tel: 01625 874225
Stockton	Graylaw House, Chestergate, Stockport SK1 1NG Tel: 0161 474 3320
Warrington	The Market Hall, Academy Way, Warrington WA1 2EN Tel: 01925 632571

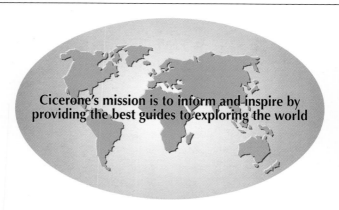

Cicerone's mission is to inform and inspire by providing the best guides to exploring the world

Since its foundation over 30 years ago, Cicerone has specialised in publishing guidebooks and has built a reputation for quality and reliability. It now publishes nearly 300 guides to the major destinations for outdoor enthusiasts, including Europe, UK and the rest of the world.

Written by leading and committed specialists, Cicerone guides are recognised as the most authoritative. They are full of information, maps and illustrations so that the user can plan and complete a successful and safe trip or expedition – be it a long face climb, a walk over Lakeland fells, an alpine traverse, a Himalayan trek or a ramble in the countryside.

With a thorough introduction to assist planning, clear diagrams, maps and colour photographs to illustrate the terrain and route, and accurate and detailed text, Cicerone guides are designed for ease of use and access to the information.

If the facts on the ground change, or there is any aspect of a guide that you think we can improve, we are always delighted to hear from you.

Cicerone Press
2 Police Square Milnthorpe Cumbria LA7 7PY
Tel:01539 562 069   Fax:01539 563 417
e-mail:info@cicerone.co.uk   web:www.cicerone.co.uk

CICERONE